Seaham
Then and Now

by

George Hoare & Ian Wright

Author George Hoare outside the house where he was born, 6 Vincent Street, Seaham. George attended Viceroy Infants, the Church of England School and Ryhope Grammar. He is now retired after 45 years in the printing trade.

Ian Wright (left) and his assistant Paul Foster. A former Sunderland AFC photographer, Ian is a partner in a reprographics company based at Seaham's Byron House.

Copyright © George Hoare & Ian Wright 1998

First published in 1998 by

The People's History
Suite 1
Byron House
Seaham Grange Business Park
Seaham
Co. Durham
SR7 0PW

ISBN 1 899560 41 6

Contents

Acknowledgements

The People's History would like to thank the following individuals who have shared their memories with us:

Joan Pace (née Hodges)
Born and brought up in Seaham, Joan not only recalls her memories of Seaham but also of her family dating back well into the last century. Her father was an official in the offices at Seaham and Vane Tempest Collieries. Joan also worked at Vane Tempest

George Forster
One of the leading lights in the Sunderland AFC Supporters' Association, George was born and bred in Seaham. This is no surprise as Seaham has always been an area from which Sunderland has drawn large and fanatical support. George recalls his early childhood in Benevente Street and wartime in Seaham when he served in the ATC.

Mick Bute
Although born in Sunderland, Mick served part of his apprenticeship at Vane Tempest. He provides a 'townies' eye view of Seaham life in the 1960s. Today Mick works on power stations all over the world. In December 1997 he wrote and published *A Town Like Alice's*, a radical re-interpretation of the role the North East played in the works of Lewis Carroll.

We would also like to thank:

John Cummings MP

Seaham Library

Michael Anderson, David Angus, Andrew Clark, Peter Gibson, Phil Hall, Adrian Marshall, Brian Marwood, Paul Nixon, Northeast Press, Jim Pace, Bob Palmer, Ed Pickford, Seaham Red Star, Sunderland Central Library, Ashley Sutherland, Alan Tedder, Margaret Thynne, Alice Willcocks, John Yearnshire

Seaham Observer
Seaham Weekly News
Shields Gazette
Sunderland Echo

London Illustrated News
Monthly Supplement of The Penny Magazine

Marwood's Maritime Directory
Pigot's Directory
Ward's Directory

THE DOCKS, SEAHAM HARBOUR.

Introduction

As the *People's History* is based in Seaham it is fitting that one of the first books in the series should feature the town. *Seaham Then and Now* is not a complete history of the town but snapshots in time. There have already been a number of excellent books on Seaham, such as *Seaham Harbour: The first 100 years 1828-1928* and *The Changing Face of Seaham 1928-1992* by Tom McNee and David Angus. Our aim is to maintain the high standard of these with this new work.

The vast majority of the pictures in *Seaham Then and Now* will be seen for the first time. Most of the old photographs are from the personal collection of George Hoare. The modern photographs were taken by Ian Wright. In many instances the old and new are placed together showing how things have changed (or not) over the years.

Advertisements from local newspapers provide an insight into everyday life in Seaham. Whether it was opportunities to emigrate, undertakers for hire or the opening of a new cricket ground, the *Seaham Observer* and *Seaham Weekly News* covered it. Another important feature of the book is the stories by local residents. Seaham-born Joan Pace and George Forster and 'Townie' Mick Bute share their memories from before the war to the present day.

For more than a century and a half the harbour and docks provided a hive of activity. For much of this period coal dominated the local economy. Shortly after the last war there were 6,260 miners in Seaham. Four out of five men in the town had jobs connected in some way with the coal industry. Today Seaham, Dawdon and Vane Tempest Collieries have all gone.

The redevelopment of the Dawdon Colliery site is underway, this will provide a link road to the A19. Homes are going up on the land where Seaham Colliery once stood, while Vane Tempest is still, as yet, undeveloped.

Leisure and sport play an important part in any community and Seaham is no exception. Picture houses, like the Cosy, provided a cheap form of entertainment. The visit of the circus was another treat for the family. The beach and the Dene also provided countless hours of free amusement.

Golf, cricket, boxing, darts, cycling and angling have all proved popular pastimes with Seaham folk over the years. However, the sport that has dominated all others has been football. Although trips were run from Seaham to see the 1932 FA Cup Final to see Newcastle United, it has been Sunderland AFC that locals have taken to their hearts. On the field Seaham has provided some great footballers. Seaham White Star and Seaham Albion were successful clubs at the turn of the century while today the top club is Seaham Red Star. After forming in the early '70s Red Star have worked their way up to the First Division of the Northern League. During this period a number of Red Star players have gone on to League football. This has maintained a long line of Seaham footballers who have moved on to the professional ranks. The list includes: George Holley, Gary Rowell, Ritchie Pitt, Terry Fenwick and Brian Marwood.

For some, public houses provide their main source of entertainment. From its earliest days, pubs have been an important part of Seaham life. The Londonderry Arms and Lord Seaham are two old hostelries which are still going strong – now known as Sylvia's and the Harbour View respectively.

Shops such Woolworths, Broxholme's and Ryles are fondly remembered by the older generation. Church Street of old can be compared with the modern day pedestrianised shopping centre.

In Parliament, Seaham has been represented by some notable figures. The early influence of the Vanes and Tempests, Sidney and Beatrice Webb, Ramsay MacDonald, Manny Shinwell and today's MP John Cummings are all featured.

The Londonderrys have already been extensively covered in books like Tony Whitehead's *The Londonderrys, Masters of Seaham*. However, they still crop up in this book as well. A number of the important visitors to Seaham were the guests of the Londonderrys.

Hard times are not unknown to Seaham: the battle to relieve poverty and disease, coal strikes and tragedies like the 1962 Lifeboat disaster, bear witness to this.

The courage of Seaham folk to overcome such hardships is a testament to their enduring spirit. This book is dedicated to those people.

OUR TOWN

Early Days of Seaham Harbour … Benevente Street … Oliver Street … Londonderry Landmarks … Wartime Memories … Going up the Ladder … The Day the Earth Shook … Schooldays … Aged Miners' Homes

Seaham Hall is one of the few buildings to have survived the transfer of power from the Milbankes to the Londonderrys early in the last century. The 'old' Seaham made way for the new town created by the Londonderry family.

Seaham Remembered

In the summer of 1930 the *Sunderland Daily Echo* shared the memories of one of Seaham's oldest residents. Mrs Mary Ann Tasker then lived in Back South Railway Street next door to her granddaughter (one of her 33 grandchildren and 37 great-grandchildren). Born on 25th November 1840 she and her husband William had five daughters and three sons. At the time of the interview Mrs Tasker had been a widow for more than fifty years.

I was born at 10 William Street, Seaham Harbour. My father Robert Thompson, came from Darlington to Seaham to 'teem' coal when the docks began.

My mother came from Pittington, and was in service at the Golden Lion Hotel, one of the first public houses opened in Seaham Harbour.

My father helped to build his own house in William Street, carrying off the beach stones for the walls.

I can remember when there were no water taps in Seaham, and when we got our water from a pump near where the Seamen's Mission now stands.

In those days the police court was held at the Lord Seaham Hotel.

I was married at the age of 17. My husband was 21.

I was left a widow early and had to bring up my family, and I have had to work hard all my life.

An early print of Seaham Harbour

Nicky Nack House

My great-grandmother used to live in the old mill (the Nicky Nack House). It is romantic today to live in a round house but my mother said it was horrible. You couldn't put a piece of furniture against the wall as all the walls were curved and sloped inward.

Joan Pace

Jane Corkhill, who lived in the
Nicky Nack House.

Benevente Street

I was born on 7th October 1926 at 22 Benevente Street, Seaham, the second son of Robert and Eleanor Forster. I had a brother Robert who was three years older than me and we were brought up by loving and caring parents.

I gather that the name of 'our street', along with Corcyra, Polemarch and others which ran off Princess Road, was named after Lord Londonderry's horses. I know that at the other side of Benevente Street, at the bottom near Grant's Crescent, the famous Sunderland footballer George Holley lived - but in my early years this meant nothing to me.

My earliest recollections of life must have been when I was about 4 years old - playing with my childhood sweetheart Mary Bowmaker in our backyard with her tea set. Then my first day at Dawdon Infants when I ran home because I did not like it and got a smack for doing so.

As well as the Bowmakers, other family friends were the Tiltmans, Littles, Shillaws and Hudsons.

George Forster

Left: George W. Forster, aged four, outside the front of 22 Benevente Street, the home of his parents Robert and Edith and elder brother Robert.

Below: Benevente Street in 1998.

The eleventh century Church of St Mary photographed in the late 1800s.
It was built at the end of the Anglo-Saxon period and the beginning of the
Norman era.

The same view of St Mary's today.

Family Bath Nights

My father was a clerk at Seaham Colliery when he was offered the job of cashier at the new Vane Tempest Colliery. He took up the position and had to work in wooden huts until the offices were built. We were given a colliery house in Oliver Street which had 3 bedrooms, living room, scullery and a bathroom. The bathroom had hot water, which was a great wonder at the time; nobody else in the family had hot water. As my father was one of 14 and my mother one of 9 quite a number used to queue up for a bath at our house. There was no shortage of hot water as father used to get coal free from the colliery. As an official he got the best quality coal: huge pieces called 'big roundies' that used to spark when put on the fire. In fact we had so much hot water we had to run it off.

Joan Pace

Mrs Adeline Hodges and daughter Joan outside 16 Oliver Street in the early thirties.

Satellite dishes are one feature that has changed in Oliver Street since the '30s.

Marlborough Street,   Seaham Harbour.

Marlborough Street in the last century.

The residents of Marlborough Street and their professions in 1899-1900 were listed in *Ward's Directory*. These included:

Mary Condron, schoolmistress, No 6
Luke Baxter, tailor, No 7
Robert Anderson, draughtsman, No 9
Patrick Lee, marine engineer, No 10
James Richardson, foreman, No 18
William Bailey, marine engineer, No 19
Richard Aisbett, accountant, No 20
John Dunn, marine engineer, No 23
George Alnwick, gentleman, No 33
George Boggon, reporter, No 34
James Burrell, town surveyor, No 35
George Hardy, general manager, No 37
John Harrison, manager, No 45

William James White, draper, No 48
William French, surgeon, No 50
Rev T. Copley, vicar, No 51
John Candlish, clerk, No 53
Lumley Fletcher, master mariner, No 56
Walter Hyslop, accountant, No 57
William Coxon, relieving officer, No 58
John Anderson, coalteemer, No 60
Robert Lynn, farmer, No 66
William Campbell, tax collector, No 68
Andrew Mather, school attendance officer, No 70
Herbert Henry, insurance agent, No 71

100% Meat

Nothing was wasted in households between the wars, with potato peelings, leftovers etc, going for pig swill. Men who kept pigs on allotments would come round the streets collecting this in barrows. When they killed a pig most of us got a little treat in the form of black pudding and sausage. I still remember those sausages, I've never had sausages like them since. They were pure meat!

Joan Pace

Charles Laughton

The great-grandparents of Hollywood star Charles Laughton lived in Seaham Harbour. Luke Conlon ran the Castlereagh Hotel with his wife in the 1880s. Their daughter Cissie moved to Scarborough and married a Mr Laughton.

Mrs Ann Burdon (centre of picture) was one of Seaham's oldest residents when she died in May 1935 at the age of 94. Born in Maryport, Ann started work at the age of 7 on a farm for 9d a week. She moved north with her parents and for a time worked at Mill House Farm, New Seaham. She married local man William Burdon. A widow for thirty years, she ended her days at Londonderry Street, Dawdon, with her daughter, Jane Gallagher.

Playtime

In the summer we would play outside games like mount-a-kitty, rounders, cricket and football. Unfortunately for us the playing fields were too far away. Many times our window was broken which would result in a scolding and a smack. My father was a handyman and would repair the damaged window. As a schoolboy my pocket money would be 6d a week. Enough to buy a comic such as *The Dandy* or *Beano*, moving on to *The Wizard, Adventure, Rover* or *Hotspur*. These would be swapped with my pals. Small conical packets of sherbet, soda lunches and dolly mixtures were our treats.

George Forster

George Forster (left) and Stan Close with the FA Cup in 1973.

The Londonderry Offices on Terrace Green were the headquarters of the Londonderry family's business empire. Built in 1857, the management of the family's coal mines, docks and railways took place from the Offices.

Right: A print showing the railway in front of the Londonderry Offices four years after its opening.

North Terrace & Londonderry Offices Seaham Harbour.

Above: The Londonderry Offices between the wars. *Below:* The same scene today.

The North Terrace with the statue of the 6th Marquess of Londonderry in front of the Offices.

The old Londonderry Offices now houses Seaham Police Station.

Wartime Memories

I was eleven years old the day war broke out and I remember my mother running out into the street where we were playing saying 'War's declared'. We thought they were going to drop bombs on us immediately and this feeling was compounded by the air-raid siren going off, when there was panic.

The following day I arrived for my first day at senior school to be told we would only be going in for half days because of the emergency. Later we did go in full time unless the air raid siren went off after midnight and then we went in at midday.

My parents decided we would sleep in the brick shelter in our yard all the time. There were bunk beds in it, with mattresses filled with chaff (corn husks). These were prickly things and were awful to sleep on. The plan to sleep permanently in the shelter lasted exactly two nights and then we went back inside and took our chances.

My uncle, Gerry Corkhill, his wife Barbara and three of their four children were killed in a raid on Seaham later in the war and this really brought the danger home to us. I have always thought it a shame no memorial to civilians killed in the war was ever erected in Seaham. Not even their graves are marked!

In 1942 I left school and started as a junior clerk at Crompton and Harrison. The firm built sections for the Mulberry Harbour used in the D-Day landings. However, at the time nobody knew what they were for.

During the war American soldiers were stationed at Seaham. They used to go to the dances we attended, like the 'hops' at the Conservative Club. They widened our horizons because they were like foreigners from outer space to us. You must understand my world did not go beyond the Low Colliery (New Seaham). To go to Seaham Harbour was an adventure. We were very localised. I think the war played a part in ending this community spirit.

Joan Pace

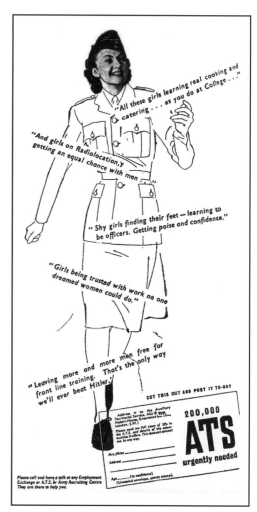

A call to join the ATS from 1941. Even teenagers had to register for youth organisations during the war. Joan Pace joined the Girls Training Corps.

16

I can see our family now sitting around the radio listening intently to the speeches of Winston Churchill. There would be complete silence and I found myself mesmerised by his voice. After Dunkirk, and the miracle of getting so many of our soldiers back home, his speeches meant so much to us. I can remember seeing the wounded and tired troops from Dunkirk on trains going north and giving them a cheer and a wave.

George Forster

Then Hermann Goering unleashed his Luftwaffe and the residents of Seaham suffered as did our neighbours Easington and Sunderland from Dorniers and Heinkels. One day when the Battle of Britain was at its height I stood on the workbench in our backyard watching the swirling vapour trails almost all around. I saw a German plane going seaward with a Hurricane (or was it a Spitfire) on its tail. It was losing height and then went out of sight. We heard later that survivors had been picked up from the sea and brought ashore to be taken away as POWs but first had to be protected from attack by angry residents.

My father was so proud of our garden that he refused to break up the carefully laid concrete paths to accommodate an air raid shelter but we were able to share the Hudson's next door. My brother and I would dread the noise of sirens and having to get out of our warm bed and on the odd occasion we would refuse. But there was a time when we were pleased to have heeded our parents' warning. One night the bombing had been severe and close. When we returned to our house after the all-clear was sounded, we found most of our ceiling was down. A huge slab of ceiling lay across our bed which could have killed us.

I was home one day with my mother when we heard the drone of a lone aircraft - a Dornier 217 I believe. I dashed outside and stood on my father's workbench with a sieve on my head. I ignored my mother's screams for me to get indoors and under the table. I watched as two objects left the plane, which I thought at first were parachutists, but they did not open. There was the sound of 'wheee' then a 'pop.' About a minute later I jumped down from the bench, opened the backgate and was then enveloped in a cloud of dust. Later we learned that two landmines had been dropped on Viceroy Street killing several people. There was another time when I witnessed a landmine on a chute hanging from a tree on the road to Dalton-le-Dale. I don't know how this was dealt with.

This was an age when most of us had bogies - a contraption of 4 wheels fixed to a plank with a box to sit on and a rope to turn the front wheels for steerage. We would take these all round the shops in Seaham collecting cardboard and paper for the war effort. I remember a bring and buy sale with goods on clippy mats outside our back door - the money raised going to the Spitfire Fund. If my memory serves me right it cost £5,000 to buy a Spitfire.

During the war I was in the Air Training Corps but by the time I was old enough I went in to the Army and by the time I'd finished training it was VE Day. I did think I would still be fighting in the Far East but then Japan surrendered.

George Forster

The First World War Memorial on Terrace Green. On the left pointing out to sea is the Russian gun from the Crimean War given to the town by Queen Victoria in 1858. This was sacrificed during the 1939-45 conflict to help the war effort.

Ben Hodges and Billy Cummings in front of the air-raid shelter in St Aldwyn Road, Seaham.

St Mary Magdalene's officially opened on 19th September 1907. The old Roman Catholic church in Tempest Place had opened in 1870 but became too small and the decision was made to replace it. Land was bought from Lord Londonderry for £500 and the total expenditure including the presbytery reached £6,000. The church was built in the Romanesque style with the stained glass from the old church transferred to the new.

Above: The School Camp on the seafront in the 1930s. During the war the huts were used by the military.

Just after the war our school bus used to pick up a boy who was squatting in one of the huts with his family.

George Hoare

Left: The camp site today.

Going up the Ladder

My mother grew up in Swinebank Cottages, Seaham, in the last century. She referred to them as Cottages Row and I think they were built for the sinkers of Seaham Colliery. They were colliery-owned and the house originally had two tenants: one up and one down. But when she lived there the family occupied it all. To get to the bedroom you had to climb a ladder. At children's bedtime you would hear, 'Come on you're going up the ladder'. This old Seaham expression is still used today by some last thing at night.

Joan Pace

The Noah's Ark in North Railway Street today. Early this century Elijah Clark ran the pub. At this time biblical names were still popular: Jeptha Ballantyne was a beer retailer in Fenwick's Row, Jabez Purdy was a grocer in South Crescent and Jeremiah Hall was a gentleman residing at Marlborough Street.

Trip Fund

Before the war my father used to run a 'trip fund' for officials at Vane Tempest. Five shillings a week was taken from their wages and paid out in the summer. Some used the money to buy something, but we had a holiday every year. In 1939 my father and mother and three children left for Redcar along with Mr and Mrs Newby and their two and Mr and Mrs Whitelock and their three. It was supposed to be for a fortnight, but on the first Friday father said 'I've just seen the newspapers. War is

Vane Tempest officials on holiday at Redcar in August 1939. Left to right: Mr Whitelock and son, Mr Hodges and son and Mr Newby.

coming and I think it's coming now'. So we packed and went home and then, on the Sunday, war was declared.

Joan Pace

Holidays

As a young boy in the 1930s, my brother and I would accompany our parents on holidays by train to our relations at Thurlaston in Leicestershire. We would go for a week or so and they would stay with us in Seaham. They simply thought the beach was the place to be: they almost had to be dragged away. When I started work I valued my weekends of leisure. I bought a lightweight bike for over £80, a fortune in those days. It was at 22 Benevente Street that we would plan Youth Hostel excursions both for weekends and annual holidays. The Lake District and the Peak District were the favourite places.

George Forster

St. Andrew's Church, Dalton-le-Dale. 7213

The twelfth century Church of St Andrew at Dalton-le-Dale.

Last Harvest Festival in Seaham Harbour United Methodist Free Church.

Early on Sunday 20th March 1904, a fire started in the United Methodist Free Church. The daughter of the caretaker raised the alarm at 2.30 am but the fire quickly spread and completely destroyed the church. The old church dated from 1866, was rebuilt in 1877 and had been renovated only three years before the fire. An appeal was immediately launched to rebuild it and within a week £348 had been raised. While building was going on services were held in Seaham Harbour Co-operative Hall. The new church, with a seating capacity of 600, was officially opened on 29th July 1905.

Seaham Harbour United Methodist Free Church after the Fire.

North Terrace from N., Seaham Harbour

68034

Above: The North Terrace with the Londonderry Offices (on left of picture) early this century.

Right: The same scene today shows the open spaces have been maintained.

Coal House, Toilet & Midden

We used to have coal delivered by horse and cart. It was emptied into the back lane and left to be shovelled through a high wooden gate into the coal house. Boys would follow the cart shouting 'Hoy your coal in for a penny Missus'. It was hard work and if possible you chose a big lad who could reach high up.

Next to the coal house was the toilet. We had a flush toilet and my mother used to hang new-mown hay in there. This was sweet smelling and acted as a deodorant.

We also had a midden, which was built into a little opening between the wall and toilet. It had a lid which lifted to allow household waste and ashes to be thrown in. The hot ashes sterilised what was in there and men came every week to empty it. Believe me, everytime I put something in my wheelie bin today I am glad. When I used to lift the lid of the midden, the smell was horrible.

Joan Pace

The Day the Earth Shook

In June 1931 some of the residents of Seaham were awakened by a mini-earthquake. Bernard Finn, landlord of the Station Hotel, recalled 'The whole house shook. The bed shook and moved up and down about half a dozen times. A chest of drawers and a wardrobe rattled up against the wall'. A police sergeant on duty in Ropery Walk was standing near a shop when it shook as if it was going to collapse. Hugh Kitson the resident of Melbourne House also felt the tremors. He said 'There was a noise like escaping steam coming out of the ground and then the whole house rocked like a cradle'.

The home of Tom and Mary Marlborough, Rutland Street, Seaham in 1951. Back: Tom Marlborough, Joan Hodges. Middle: Mary Marlborough, Adeline Hodges, Ben Hodges snr. Front: Ben Hodges jnr. The old colliery fire range can be seen on the right.

Londonderry Road between the wars. At one time almost every street and road in Seaham was given a name connected with the Londonderry family.

The Marchioness of Londonderry School, Church Street

I went to this school from about 1942 until 1946. It was attacked during the war and the roof damaged by machine-gun fire. For a while we had to share our school with the Ropery Walk School on a half day basis, going one week on the mornings and the next on afternoons. On one of the afternoons I had off, I saw a lone bomber come over. It dropped a mine on a parachute which landed near Seaham Colliery.

George Hoare

A print from 1858.

Camden Square

I failed my 11 Plus, I really thought I'd done better than I had. A lot of my pals went to Ryhope Grammar School while I went to Camden Square Intermediate School. Teachers there included: Miss Burgess (English), Miss Laws (Music), 'Conkie' Clark (Maths, Woodwork & Sport), Mr 'Pop' Robson (History) and Mr Cunningham (Head). They were good teachers. The lessons of Mr Robson, an ex shell-shocked veteran, were enthralling and gave me a great pride in being British. In Maths you had to know your times table - there were no calculators in those days. At Sport I was really good at running but Wilf Shillaw just had the edge.

George Forster

Low Colliery School

I went to the Low Colliery School in Station Road before the last war. The school was demolished and is now an industrial site. There was a coal fire at the front of the class and this was an incentive to work hard at your studies. The cleverest pupils were placed at the front of the class. There were half a dozen teachers at the school and a headmistress who was never afraid to wield the stick for anything. I remember Miss Dixon, the reception class teacher, encouraged her young pupils to have a short sleep in the afternoon. She also took the opportunity to sleep. She was a good teacher and was nice and kind.

Joan Pace

Princess Road Junior School was formerly Seaham Harbour Girls' Grammar School.

Viceroy Street Infants. The school was built at the end of the last century and will be fondly remembered by thousands who started their education there. The street after which the school was named was in turn named after a relative of the first Marquess of Londonderry who was Viceroy of Ireland.

A Viceroy Street class in the days when hundreds of children attended the school. The school only had a couple of dozen pupils or so in 1972 when it closed.

The wedding of Jim Pace and Joan
Hodges at Christ Church, Seaham
9th August 1952.

Joan and Jim Pace, August 1992. Jim
is a well-known local historian and
photographer.

Hall Street at the time of the First World War.

The back yard of one of the Castlereagh Aged Miners' Homes, North Road. George and Agnes Arthur, and granddaughter, Pat, pose for the camera in the 1930s.

The Homes were built to commemorate the 21st birthday of Viscount Castlereagh. On 19th December 1923 the Marquess of Londonderry's son laid the foundation stone of the dozen houses. He then made the short journey to cut the first turf of Vane Tempest Colliery.

Dating from the middle of the last century, the Londonderry Institute in Tempest Road was converted into 16 flats in 1994 by the Durham Aged Mineworkers' Homes Association.

St. John's (Parish Church), Seaham Harbour

Above: An old view of St John's Church. *Below:* The same scene today. The church opened on 7th June 1840. The following year a bazaar organised by the Marchioness of Londonderry raised £1,200 for the church.

Seaside Sundays

My mother, whilst not a religious fanatic, was a regular attender at St John's Church and she made sure that her two sons regularly went to church and Sunday school. On odd occasions we'd 'doll-off', spending our penny collection money on sweets then going to the seashore – dodging the waves. We'd have our Sunday best on. Somehow she would always find out, perhaps by the giveaway salt marks on our shoes.

George Forster

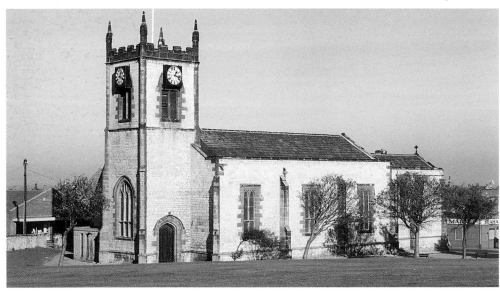

SECTION TWO

THAT'S ENTERTAINMENT

Princess Theatre … Age of Elegance at the Theatre Royal …
Werewolf at the Empire … Cosy Memories … Sanger's Circus …
From Seaham to Covent Garden … Monster Picnic … Jubilee
Pleasure Gardens … The Stud Farm

DAWDON DENE, SEAHAM HARBOUR

Entertainment could not come any cheaper than a stroll in the Dene.

Princess Theatre

Film shows at the Princess Theatre provided cheap entertainment for thousands of families in the Dawdon area.

In her book *Happy Days*, Alice Willcocks recalled 'I loved the Princess. I always had five or six children with me. We used to buy penny bars of toffee which we broke fairly easily across the back of the seats into equal sized pieces along the grooves and so we could all get a bit. At that time the houses on the east side of Princess Road had not been built, there were just mounds of earth and grass, so on our way home we would run up and down these mounds shouting our heads off just like the cowboys in the picture we had seen.'

When the Princess closed as a cinema it opened as a bingo hall. The building that provided so many happy memories is now demolished.

THIS is a reproduction of a 'snap' of the Princess Cinema, where the most up-to-date pictures are always shewn, twice nightly at 6.45 and 8.45.

YOU should make a point of always visiting this theatre, it will be an evening exceedingly well spent. Prices of admission are :— Circle, 9d. Pit Stalls, 6d. Pit, 4d. — or you can secure a most comfortable box for a very small sum.

Princess Theatre
~ DAWDON ~
SEAHAM ~ HARBOUR.

An advert for the Princess in the 1920s when admission prices ranged from 4d to 9d.

PRINCESS THEATRE
DAWDON, SEAHAM HARBOUR.

MONDAY, SEPTEMBER 7th, 1914.

Sunday, Monday, Tuesday and Wednesday,

BY SPECIAL REQUEST.

SIXTY YEARS
A QUEEN

The Life of Queen Victoria—in 7 Parts.

GREAT PATRIOTIC PROGRAMME!

Thursday, Friday and Saturday,

WAR IN BELGIUM

Shewing how the Brave Belgians resisted the Kaiser's Legions.

FIRST TIME HERE! EXCLUSIVE!

THE WAR CORRESPONDENT

A Thrilling Episode of the present War.

NOTICE—Owing to the enormous length of these Pictures no Turns have been engaged for this Week.

The outbreak of World War One signalled a flood of patriotic films in cinemas. A month after hostilities began the Princess Theatre was showing scenes of the invasion of Belgium.

Theatre Royal & Golden Lion Hotel.

(A. C. HARRISON, Proprietor)

An advert for the Theatre Royal and Golden Lion in the 1920s

Age of Elegance

Mr Harrison used to stand in front of the Theatre Royal in evening dress, greeting everybody as they entered. I remember one pantomime there when a lady swung out over the audience on a swing. Everybody was frightened she would come off and land on them.

Joan Pace

Theatre Royal

The Theatre Royal closed in 1961 but even then it had been kept opened by AC Harrison longer than made economic sense. As films replaced variety theatre, bingo was the new form of entertainment the people wanted and it became a bingo hall.

On the site of the Theatre Royal now stands the Co-op supermarket.

Empire Theatre

Built in 1912, the Empire Theatre was soon showing silent films with favourites like Laurel and Hardy, Buster Keaton and Charlie Chaplin.

The Empire was modernized just before the last war. The ornate facade on top of the building was replaced with a style in vogue in the thirties.

The last film shown at the Empire was *South Pacific* on 31st August 1968.

Right: An advert for the Empire Theatre from the early 1920s before alterations.

Classic films showing at the Empire in January 1936.

Today the Empire Theatre with the 'For Sale' signs up.

Werewolf of Seaham

The Empire used to change its film programme twice a week. I got mixed up and instead of seeing a romantic film I saw *The Werewolf*. I was absolutely terrified. I saw a neighbour, Ronnie Peel, sitting with his coat over his head. He turned round and saw me and scrambled over the seats and said 'Joan do you mind if I sit beside you, I'm terrified'. I was over the moon to say 'Yes'. We came out after the film and he said 'Do you mind if we walk up the road together'. I welcomed the company because it was wartime and with the black out there was no street lighting. The only light was at the station and as we were passing the gaslight began to splutter. We shot off, running all the way home. My mother would not let me go to the pictures alone for a year. I had nightmares for ages after.

Joan Pace

Cosy Memories

Jam Jars

I remember as a child in the 1930s we used to pay 6d to sit in the front rows of the pictures. We would go to the Princess, Empire or Royal and come out with stiff necks. But we could get in at the Cosy in New Seaham on a Saturday afternoon with a couple of jam jars to watch a matinee performance to see Tom Mix or Flash Gordon.

George Forster

The site in Stockton Road where the Cosy once stood.

The Cosy

The Cosy was a purpose built cinema and had no upstairs. The more expensive seats were still at the back. Some people went to the pictures every night but we just went once, or for a treat, twice a week. Today new houses stand near Seaton View Nursing Home where the Cosy used to be.

Joan Pace

Tobacco Health Warning

Picture house patrons before the last war unwittingly provided the raw material for a tobacco scam. The *Seaham Weekly News* of 24th April 1936 reported on a court case in Clerkenwell, London. The firm of Nicall Products Ltd were fined £300 and costs for 'manufacturing tobacco without an excise licence.' Found in a secret room in the factory was 500 lb of sweepings from cinemas comprising cigarette ends, chocolate wrappers and used matches. The tobacco was sorted by girls and made into cigarettes or sold loose inscribed with the 'seal of quality' label. On average 3 lb of tobacco was retrieved from every $4^1/_2$ lb of sweepings. The court heard how sweepings were collected from cinemas by a traveller called Mr Veal. In the last four months of 1935 he collected 2,000 lb of sweepings at 3d or 4d a lb. He then sold it on for 6d a lb. The tobacco manufactured from the sweepings was sold for 8 shillings a lb and cigarettes at 16 shillings a lb.

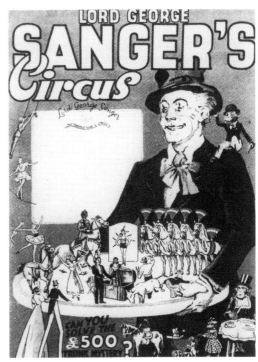

Lord George Sanger's Circus performed at Seaham at Easter 1905. A field farmed by J.W. Dryden was hired for the occasion.

Left: An advert for the Good Friday performance at Seaham.

A special meeting of Seaham Harbour Branch of the Church of England Men's Society was held at the Oddfellows' Hall to protest against Sanger's Circus performing on Good Friday. They expressed their outrage at the desecration of the 'most sacred and solemn day in the whole year'. A meeting at the Drill Hall attended by 1,500 people also passed a resolution condemning the circus.

Although the circus was being held at New Seaham the fact that the procession passed through Seaham Harbour brought the protests. This showed the different attitudes the two communities held on the question of entertainment on Good Friday. On the same day as the circus performance Seaham Albion played a football match at New Seaham.

GROWN WITH
HADFIELD'S
SPECIAL TURNIP
MANURE
BY Mr J.H.DRYDEN
SEAHAM HARBOUR

An excellent crop, weighing nearly 40 tons per acre.

Sanger's big top was pitched in a field on Dryden's farm. Dryden leased the land he farmed from the North-Eastern Railway Company.
Above and below: Two advertisement cards in which J. Dryden endorses the qualities of Hadfield's Special Turnip Manure.

GROWN WITH
HADFIELD'S
SPECIAL TURNIP
MANURE
BY Mr J.DRYDEN
SEAHAM HARBOUR
SUNDERLAND

Mr. DRYDEN says—I used **5** cwts. per acre on these Turnips, and they turned out a splendid crop, weighing **38** tons per acre. They started early and resisted the wet well, and were fine feeding when pulled.

Seaham Harbour Salvation Army Band in Liverpool at Easter 1932.

Band on the Prom

One of the entertainments on offer at Seaham in the summer of 1874 was supplied by the Londonderry Workshop Band. They performed on the North Terrace and Promenade every Thursday evening. The programme for the 2nd July included:

March	Vacant Chair
Quadrille	Clyde
Overture	Slave
Polka	London Bells
March	Mountaineer
Waltz	Forest Fairies
Schottische	Mountain Belle
Finale	God Save The Queen

From Seaham to Covent Garden

World famous opera singer Thomas Allen was born in Seaham. After studying at the Royal College of Music from 1964 to 1968 the baritone worked his way to the top. He has appeared at the Royal Opera House, Covent Garden; the Metropolitan, New York; La Scala, Milan and Glyndebourne.

In his book *Foreign Parts: A Singer's Journal*, Thomas recalled with affection his early days in Seaham. Today, in his spare time, he enjoys drawing and painting. Vane Tempest Colliery and Parkside Allotments have been some of his subjects.

Thomas Allen

Most people in Seaham will have heard Thomas Allen sing - he performed on the Number One hit *Perfect Day* alongside artistes like Elton John, David Bowie and Tom Jones.

A Great Soprano

The Free Church in Church Street used to stage concerts during the war. One of the most celebrated performers was Isobel Baillie. The great soprano stayed at the home of Mr and Mrs George Green in Antrim Gardens during her stay at Seaham. On one occasion, I met her, when I had to deliver a message to her on my bike. She was an absolutely lovely lady. George Green, who was a magnificent pianist, used to accompany her in numbers like *Oh Silver Moon*.

The Old Vic came to Dawdon Miners Welfare Hall around 1940. We were taken from school to see a performance of *The Merchant of Venice*. I have great memories of the visit and it gave me a love of Shakespeare which remains with me to this day.

Joan Pace

Seaham Harbour from the Dean.

A view of the Dene in 1858.

Ice Rescue

On 2nd March 1929, five-year-old Joseph Holley fell into a partly frozen pond in the Dene. Thomas Taylor (aged 12) went to his rescue but lost consciousness in the icy waters. Members of the Sea Scouts: Foster Brown, Robert Wild, Harry Watson and David Roberts rushed to the pond and got both boys out. When Thomas regained consciousness his first words were 'How is the little 'un. I tried to save him'. Both boys recovered after treatment.

The Dene from North Road, Seaham Harbour

Gardens laid out in the Dene at the end of the last century.

An advert for a 'Monster Picnic' organised by Seaham Chemical Works Reading Institute from the *Seaham Observer* of 19th June 1869. Some of the attractions were the Bottleworks' Brass Band, athletic sports and dancing.

The Bengal Gardens advertised in the *Seaham Observer* of 28th August 1869. Proprietor Robert Graydon's plans for the Gardens in Dawdon Dene received a set back when his application for an alcohol licence was rejected.

Dawdon Dene Gone "DRY" 5305

Dating from the last century, the drinking fountain in the Dene was a target for a local wit.

Jubilee Pleasure Gardens

The Jubilee Pleasure Gardens opened in the Dene on Whit Monday 1897. For several years prior, Mr Smelt, the farmer of Dalton-le-Dale, allowed school parties to use his field for picnics. The manager of the Seaham and Sunderland Railway saw the commercial possibilities and approached Lord Londonderry's agents about the venture. Mr Brydon was given the job of putting this into practice. A pavilion was built to serve tea and swings and amusements erected. The price of admission was $1\frac{1}{2}$d for children and 2d for adults.

Above: Dawdon Dene as it looked between the wars.
Right: The same scene today.

Rifle Range

Seaham and District Rifle Range opened in the Dene on 29th May 1911. Lady Londonderry performed the official opening when she fired the first shot. The range was on land leased from Mr Brydon.

Below: Gardens in the Dene.

The Stud Farm in Dawdon Dene. Robert Brydon had set up the stud at Dalden Hall in 1870 for the Londonderrys. In 1900 this was taken over by a limited company - Seaham Harbour Stud Company. The stud became famous worldwide for breeding Clydesdales. Many of these horses could also be seen on the streets of Seaham pulling the carts of various tradesmen.

Stud Farm

Seaham Harbour Stud Company staged their spring sale of Clydesdales on 4th April 1902. Before the sale a luncheon was held in a marquee belonging to Samuel Paterson Thompson of the Castlereagh Hotel.

A stallion called Sir Anthony brought the top price in the sale when the Northern Stud Company paid out 250 guineas. A total of over three thousand pounds changed hands as 61 horses found new homes.
Right: The prices the horses fetched.

	Guineas
10 brood mares	533
4 three-year-old fillies	143
1 two-year-old filly	25
4 yearling fillies	123
7 yearling colts	252
7 two-year-old colts	413
5 stallions	458
12 geldings	719
7 trained cobs & c., for saddle & harness	194
4 registered pony mares	109
Total	**2969**

In 1910 Robert Brydon regained control of the stud he had originally started. When he died, a dispersal sale was held on 7th October 1915. The 102 lots raised a total of £21,252 (a staggering sum at the time). Bonnie Buchlyvie was described by the auctioneer as 'the greatest Clydesdale horse in the world' and bidding started at 3,000 guineas. The prize stallion was finally bought for 5,000 guineas.

HARBOUR AND DOCKS

Murder in the Docks ... Coal Staithes ... The Grand Design ... The Harbour in the 1860s ... Steamers to the Tees ... Fishing boats today ... New Lighthouse and Piers ... Age of Sail ... Wartime Target

North Dock, Seaham Harbour

Seaham Harbour's old North Dock around the time of the First World War when sailing ships worked alongside steamers.

Murder in the Docks

As the year 1901 drew to a close, the inhabitants of Seaham were shocked to learn of a murder on board a ship in the docks. Trouble started when crew members, who had been drinking ashore, returned to their ships. The mate of the *Cornucopia* was attacked by a number of rowdy seamen. Frederick Terry mate of the *Tille E* went to his aid. To do this he crossed over the deck of another ship the *James Simpson* which lay between the two vessels. Once the rumpus had ended and Terry was returning to his ship he was stabbed in the back and fatally wounded.

An inquest was held at the Castlereagh Hotel where a jury returned a verdict of 'wilful murder' on the 26-year-old mate from Faversham. Three Swedish seamen appeared in court charged with assaulting the mate of the *Cornucopia* and were fined 5s and costs. At the same hearing, 23-year-old Norwegian Wilhelm Johannsen was charged with murder and remanded to appear at Durham Assizes.

In February 1902 Johannsen, a seaman on the *James Simpson*, was found guilty of murder and sentenced to death. However, the jury recommended mercy because of his youth and the sentence was commuted to life imprisonment.

An early view of Seaham Harbour.

A coal staith at Seaham Harbour in the early 1830s. By 1837, 370,000 tons of coal a year was being shipped out from the Rainton and South Hetton collieries. In the late 1970s the railways monopolised the trade and the staithes were demolished.

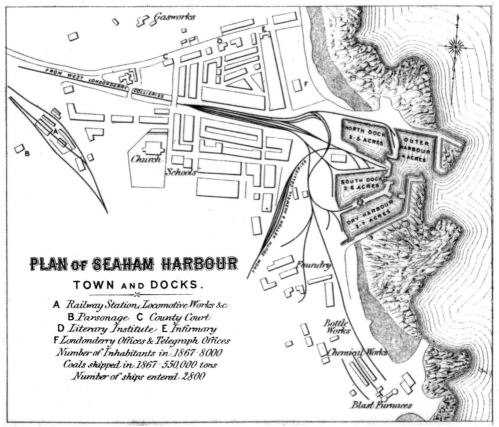

A plan showing Seaham Harbour *circa* 1867.

The Grand Design

Seaham Harbour was built by the Marquess of Londonderry between 1828 and 1831. The reason behind the scheme was to save the Marquess £10,000 a year - the cost of sending coal from his collieries from the Wear.

THE First-Class Steamer OCEAN BRIDE will leave the Quay, Seaham Harbour, for Hartlepool and Middlesbro', at Eight o'clock every Sunday morning, returning the same evening.—Tickets may be had at the 'Observer' Office, and of Mr. ROBERT FIELD.

An advert for steam boat trips from Seaham to Teesside in 1863.

The coal staithes with a sailing ship tied up alongside.

Seaham Harbour catered for all sizes and types of vessels. Cobles moored in the old Dock were once a common sight.

Today fishing boats take refuge in the old Dock.

The new lighthouse was built out of steel and opened in 1905.

A sailing ship leaves the North Dock early this century.

Sailing vessels came in all shapes and sizes.

The old pier and lighthouse. By the end of the nineteenth century the old Docks could no longer cope with the ever-expanding coal trade.

An aerial view of Seaham Harbour in the late 1940s. Ships are lined up waiting to be loaded up with coal.

THE DOCKS, SEAHAM HARBOUR.   G.7448

A ship being loaded at the coal staithes. Shipments of coal from Seaham Harbour began in July 1831 and by the end of that year 388 vessels had been loaded with coal there.

SOUTH DOCK, SEAHAM HARBOUR. 1900.

For most of this century coal was Seaham's major export. This fact and the close proximity of the collieries made the town a target for enemy bombers during the Second World War. Seaham was one of the hardest hit towns in County Durham. Between August 1940 and May 1943, hundreds of buildings were damaged or destroyed. A total of 52 people lost their lives and a further 224 were injured.

Above and below: Ships entering and leaving Seaham Harbour before the war.

Right: Seaham Harbour today.

The Docks, Seaham Harbour. 9504

WORK

*Railway Age … Hard Times at Seaham Colliery … Freezing
Dawdon … Cavilling Day at Vane Tempest … The Coffee Pot …
Wight's Iron Works … Co-op Cartman … Richards the Printers …
Byron's Legacy*

Computers at work on the Seaham Grange Industrial Estate. Since the decline
of traditional industries like mining, a wide range of new industries have been
attracted to the town.

South Hetton Railway

Colonel Braddyll, owner of South Hetton Colliery, constructed the rail link with Seaham to transport his coal to the outside world. In 1833 the first shipment of coal from the colliery arrived at Seaham Docks.

The final stretch of the South Hetton railway line running down to Seaham Harbour.

THE MARQUIS OF LONDONDERRY COMMENCING THE SEAHAM AND SUNDERLAND RAILWAY.

A print from the *London Illustrated News* showing the 3rd Marquess of Londonderry pushing a wheelbarrow with the first piece of turf signalling the start of work on the Seaham and Sunderland Railway on 8th February 1853. The need for the usual Act of Parliament for the railway was unnecessary as the Marquess owned most of the land on which it was to be built. The Marquess died before his rail link with Sunderland was complete. In August 1854 coal traffic began on the line and the following year a passenger service began.

Seaham Colliery

Seaham Colliery first produced coal in 1852. Twelve years later it amalgamated with the older Seaton Colliery. Legislation had been passed which required collieries to have two shafts. As the collieries were only a short distance apart it was easier to buy Seaton out and join them underground than going to the expense of sinking a new shaft.

In its early years Seaham Colliery was rocked by a series of explosions culminating in the disaster of 8th September 1880 which claimed 164 men and boys.

A tin water bottle belonging to one of the men who died was later recovered. While trapped and with no hope of rescue he scratched a last message to his wife on the bottle with a nail.

Dear Margaret, There was 40 of (us) altogether at 7 am. Some was singing hymns, but my thoughts was on my little Michael that him and I would meet in heaven at the same time. Oh Dear Wife, God save you and the children, and pray for me. Dear wife Farewell. My last thoughts are about you and the children. Be sure and learn the children to pray for me. Oh what an awful position we are in.

Michael Smith, 54 Henry Street.

The 'little Michael' referred to was his eighteen-month-old son who was so ill he was not expected to survive when his father went out to work on the ill-fated day. Little Michael died on the day of the explosion.

Christ Church, where the memorial to the victims of the 1880 disaster was erected.

The memorial to the 164 miners killed at Seaham Colliery in 1880. Nearby is another memorial to the 26 killed in an explosion nine years before.

A Hard Life

After starting in the tin mines in Cornwall at the age of eight, John James Fenner and his family came north the following year and young John started work at Seaham Colliery. This was around 1870 and for the next sixty years or so he worked at the colliery first as a trapper boy, then a driver, putter, timber leader, stonemason, coal hewer and for the final 45 years as a deputy overman – retiring at the grand old age of seventy.

Shortly after his arrival at Seaham, an explosion killed 26 men and boys at the colliery. Then in the 1880 disaster he lost both his father and a brother. John had been working on another shift at the time of the explosion. Tragedy struck again when another brother was killed at the colliery.

A view of Dawdon Colliery. Work started on sinking the shaft at Dawdon in August 1899 but problems arose when a bed of quicksand was reached. Thousands of gallons of water were rushing into the workings every minute. Work only continued when the surrounding ground was frozen by a series of pipes. Due to the problems of sinking, coal production was not properly underway until 1907.

From its earliest days Dawdon had a reputation for union activism. In 1929 the Lodge refused to accept a reduction in piece rates and 4,000 were locked out. Two years later 2,400 men and boys were idle at the colliery because of slackness of trade.

The Townies

I started at Vane Tempest Colliery in 1961 after spending a full year at college sponsored by the Coal Board. I did my CPS (Close Personal Supervision) under Tommy Dale the pitman poet. Tommy was always asked to recite his poems whilst waiting for the cage by the shafts going on or coming off.

I travelled on the bus from Park Lane with Geordie Taylor, another 'townie'. Townie was the name given to any person from outside the colliery community. Rather than being regarded as an outsider, there was a great camaraderie at the Tempest and you were always 'one of the lads'.

Old Ces, the labourer in the Mechanics shed, on hearing my name was Bute said 'You'll be alright here, one of the B's'. What he meant by B's was that the Unit Engineer was Bob Batey, Underground Engineer Bob Baxter, Foreman Sid Beer and his son Norman Beer, the two tradesmen I worked under were Don Beezer and Ronnie Burrell and another townie apprentice in the Mech Shed was Alan Birtley who later became Colliery Engineer. Funnily enough years later, when I was writing a book on the works of Lewis Carroll, I reflected on Vane Tempest after reading one of Carroll's so-called nonsense verses where the ship's crew all begin with B.

Mick Bute

An aerial view of Vane Tempest.

Cavilling Day

In 1943 I started work as a junior typist at the Vane Tempest offices. I sometimes helped prepare the wages bills, as in those days, we had to work out the men's taxes and 'offtakes' (deductions). If the man was a Catholic, 'priest money' came off his wage slip. This was not for the priest himself, but for the upkeep of the Roman Catholic Church in Seaham.

The big event of the year was Cavilling Day. This was when men were allocated the different seams and districts in which they would work. We used to go in early in the morning and every man's name was written on a piece of paper to be drawn out of a hat. This was done by the under manager and cashier, for the colliery owners, and the checkweighman acted as the men's representative. A cheer would go up if the man got a good district but a moan was heard if a bad one.

Joan Pace

Blacksmiths' Shop

Any Monday morning a group would be warming their backsides in Vane Tempest's Blacksmiths' Shop around Paddy Lennox's fire. Paddy was the Mechanics Union Secretary in those days, though he left later to take over as Steward at Sunderland Catholic Club. In the winter, however, some of the discussions on football and other topics would be interrupted by a large snowball being dropped down the furnace flue, scattering everyone from the splutter and steam. They were all blacksmiths of the old school: Foreman Harry Robson and his son Terry, Joe Dyer, Frankie Smith, Paddy Lennox and his striker Val.

Mick Bute

Vane Tempest office staff around 1936.

Built around 1873, the Coffee Pot steam locomotive was still in use in the docks almost a century later.

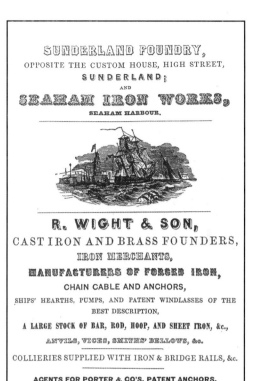

An advert from *Marwood's Maritime Directory* of 1848 for Wight's Iron Works.

Anchorsmiths vs Forgemen

At Easter 1870 a coble race was held between anchorsmiths and forgemen employed at Wight's Ironworks. A fine day and calm seas drew a crowd of 2,000 to watch the race. The anchorsmiths' coble the *Victory* and the forgemen's vessel the *Volunteer* set off from near Ryhope Dene at 3 o'clock in the afternoon. The five-man crews kept pace with each other all the way to Seaham. But it was the anchorsmiths who crossed the finishing line opposite the pier first. They won by a distance of 3 lengths in a time of 20 minutes 45 seconds. Referee John Chilton of the Braddyll Arms handed over the sidestake of £10 to the winning team.

Ouija board

A lot of pranks were played at bank (on the surface) at Vane Tempest Colliery and I think this compensated for the strict observation of the Mines & Quarries Act underground. One which I was not a witness to, was related to me by Electrician Stan Crosby. Don Beezer was at the centre of things when he had a group assemble around a ouija board in the Lamp Cabin. Don had arranged for someone on the roof to hold cat-gut which was tied to the chairs in the cabin.

As the would-be seance members all touched a glass in the centre of the ouija board Don released a mouse from the palm of his hand. As it ran across the board someone shouted 'It's an omen', did a sign of the cross and ran for the door. As the others followed, the guy on the roof started to make the chairs dance. Don fell about as the others tried to pull each other back to get out of the cabin first.

Mick Bute

Mick Bute in 1998 with a copy of his book *A Town Like Alice's*. This explores the influence the region had on the works of Lewis Carroll.

Co-op Cartman

Between the wars, when times were hard, my father was fortunate to have a job at the Ryhope and Silksworth Co-operative store at Dawdon where he worked as a cartman. Orders were taken at the beginning of the week, the goods were then beautifully wrapped in brown paper and then delivered. He would take groceries by horse and cart round the district of Seaham and as far as Easington (which required 2 horses). He had one of the bigger draught horses at the Co-op called 'Dick', I don't know how many hands high he was but to a youngster he was huge. The odd occasion when off school I would accompany him on his round and he would share his malt bread date sandwiches and coffee served in a pewter can. I can remember having a peep at my father's wage packet just before the war and it was £2 7s 6d (£2 37$^{1}/_{2}$p).

George Forster

The Divi

In April 1931 membership of the Ryhope and Silksworth Co-operative Society stood at 17,106. Sales for the six months period which had just ended amounted to £310,261. This was slightly down on the previous half year's figures but this was put down to a fall in prices of the principal commodities and the 'unsatisfactory industrial position'.

One of the reasons for this customer loyalty was the 'dividend' paid out on each sale. This was eventually phased out in the 1960s and replaced with Co-op stamps. But these in turn lost their popularity and the scheme ended.

In March 1998 the North East Co-op revived the dividend scheme in their stores. For every £1 spent on Co-op goods customers get 5p. Twice a year customers can receive cash, vouchers or donate their divi to charity.

The delivery horse and cart of Morris the Grocers in 1908. Stores like the Co-op used similar transport to deliver goods to customers' doors.

The Co-operative store at Dawdon in its heyday in the 1920s. Opposite stands the old Dawdon Workmen's Club.

The Co-operative store building at Dawdon today is used as small factory units. Opposite stands the new Dawdon Workmen's Club. Beyond the club used to stand the Princess Theatre.

The composing room of Richards the Printers in North Terrace at the turn of the century. One of the jobs of apprentice George Henry West (right) was to get beer in a billy can for the foreman (third from left) to wash the lead dust away.

Right: Today's equivalent of a composing room - a reprographics studio in Byron House on Seaham Grange Industrial Estate.

Appropriately the Byrons have a connection with modern computers. Byron enjoyed calling his wife the 'Princess of Parallelograms' because of her gift for mathematics and science. Their daughter, Ada Augusta, inherited her mother's talents. In 1833 she met Charles Babbage who was developing a calculating machine which was the forerunner of today's computers. Ada put forward the idea of using punch cards to give instructions and storing information (memory). She was the world's first computer programmer. Babbage called Ada the 'Enchantress of Numbers'.

SECTION FIVE

RED LETTER DAYS

Byron's Wedding … Disraeli visits … A Prince and the Cup at the Drill Hall … King Zog Drops in … Autogyro Sighting … Cup Final Ref … Balfour opens New South Dock … Rhodes about Seaham … Duke of Wellington

The 'Red Letter Day' for Seaham's Harry Nattrass was 25th April 1936 when he refereed the FA Cup Final at Wembley.

Seaham Hall

The Milbanke family bought the manor of Seaham in the seventeenth century. Seaham Hall dates from the early 1790s when it was commissioned by Ralph and Judith Milbanke. The couple had one child Annabella (christened Anne Isabella).

Right: Seaham Hall in the middle of the last century.

Seaham Hall, Church & Vicarage

On 2nd January 1815 Annabella married Lord Byron in the Drawing Room of Seaham Hall. During his brief stay at Seaham, Byron worked on *The Hebrew Melodies* and The *Siege of Corinth*. These are acknowledged as some of the poet's finest works.

Lady Byron

Lord Byron

Seaham Hall Sanatorium. 7329

During the First World War Seaham Hall served as an Auxiliary War Hospital. Local picture houses used to give free tickets to the recuperating servicemen.

In 1927 Seaham Hall became a tuberculosis sanatorium.

On 8th December 1861 Disraeli wrote from Seaham Hall: 'This is a remarkable place, and our hostess is a remarkable woman. Twenty miles hence she has a palace (Wynyard) in a vast park, with forest rides and antlered deer, with all the accessories of feudal life. But she prefers living in a hall on the shores of the German Ocean (North Sea), surrounded by her collieries and her blast furnaces, and her rail roads, and the unceasing telegraphs, with a port hewn out of the solid rock, screw steamers and four thousand pitmen under her control. One day she dined the whole 4,000 in one of her factories.

Benjamin Disraeli

Today in 1998 there are plans to turn Seaham Hall into a hotel and restaurant.

King Edward VII

King Edward VII stayed at Wynyard in October 1903 on a shooting holiday. He was due to visit Seaham Harbour but the trip was cancelled due to torrential rain, much to the disappointment of the large crowds that had gathered. As Prince of Wales he had been the guest of the Londonderrys on a number of occasions and visited the Harbour on 1st November 1890. That day the crowds drawn to Seaham to see the Prince and Princess were estimated at between fifty and eighty thousand. The Royal couple arrived at Seaham Harbour Station to find almost every house in the town decorated in some way. One of the places of interest visited was the Drill Hall which had opened only two years before to house the Seaham Volunteer Artillery Brigade.

King Edward VII

Coronation & FA Cup

A Coronation Ball was held at the Drill Hall on 12th May 1937. The 470 guests toasted the start of George VI's reign. Players and officials of Sunderland AFC were guests of honour and brought along the FA Cup which they had won a few days before. Manager Johnny Cochrane said 'We came here tonight to show our appreciation of the many supporters we have at Seaham, because we find we have more supporters from Seaham than from any other county town in Durham'. Accompanying Cochrane were trainer Andy Reid and players Raich Carter, Jimmy Gorman, Bert Johnston, Patsy Gallacher and Len Duns.

King Zog Drops In

In the 1930s my mother bought a beautiful coffee set. It was bright green with gold dragons. When my father came home she said, 'Look what I've bought'. He said 'What do you want a coffee set for? We don't even drink coffee'. She replied 'You never know who will come'. He thought it was pure extravagance but it stood on the sideboard and was my mother's pride and joy.

King Zog with silk handkerchief.

Then one day King Zog of Albania came to Vane Tempest for a visit. My father was an official and brought him to our house to show him how British workers lived. My mother's coffee set was then used for the first and only time. We were banished to the scullery but I can still remember the smell of the coffee. It still brings back memories when I make coffee today. King Zog gave my father a pure silk handkerchief which he always wore in his top pocket.

Joan Pace

Seaham sees an Autogyro

In 1931 or 1932, whilst I was a pupil at Byron Terrace School, I was in the playground when all play ceased. Everyone gazed in wonder at a strange aircraft flying low overhead. It was an autogyro, the forerunner of today's helicopter. It was the

invention of a Spaniard, Senor La Cierva, and almost certainly he was the pilot. Sadly, he died in 1936 when the aircraft in which he was travelling (not an autogyro) crashed in England.

Jim Pace

Christmas Day

On Christmas Day we were fortunate to get good toys. I had a wonderful collection of lead soldiers and farmyard animals. Later years our treat was a Hornby clockwork (our house did not have electricity just gas) train set. A Meccano set which was added to over the years was another super present. A large wooden rocking horse was kept along with other toys in the box-room (spare room) where we'd spend many happy hours in the winter months.

George Forster

Cup Final Ref

New Seaham's Harry Nattrass achieved the pinnacle as a football referee when he took charge of the 1936 FA Cup Final. The amazing thing about this achievement was the fact that he was only in his second season as a League referee.

He was a regular spectator at Roker Park before taking up refereeing in 1921. He worked his way up through the Seaham and District League, Houghton League, Wearside League, North-Eastern League and then the Football League, first as a linesman and then referee.

He had already been in charge of internationals: Scotland v Ireland, Ireland v Wales and an inter-League match, when informed he would referee the Cup Final. However, it was still a big shock to the 38-year-old Seaham man. On being told he said 'Is it really true?' When he had time to take everything in he reflected 'It is a great honour which I did not expect, being comparatively a young referee, but you can rest assured that I shall carry out my duties to the best of my ability, and try to uphold the best traditions of previous North-East referees who have officiated'.

In the Final a single goal from Ted Drake gave an all-star Arsenal side victory over Sheffield United. The Seaham man's big occasion was witnessed by 93,384 people at Wembley Stadium. The following season he would not have been able to take up the honour – Sunderland reached the Final.

Harry Nattrass poses in his referee kit with an old fashioned 'casey'. In Harry's day, officials wore blazers and shirt. Today's footballs have little in common with those of the pre-war era. The lightweight footballs of the modern game do not absorb water like those of the past, which were a nightmare for players.

Harry Nattrass being congratulated by workmates at Vane Tempest on his appointment as Cup Final referee. Today there are calls for professional referees but as yet we still have amateur officials. Trying to fit a refereeing career with full time work cost Harry Nattrass his job shortly before his Cup Final appointment. After working as a miner at Seaham Colliery and Vane Tempest for 25 years, he was given his notice. Although football was not given as the reason for his notice he was informed off the record that this was the cause. In the previous close season he had never lost a shift but league and international fixtures severely affected his attendance at work during the football season.

Premier Visit

Prime Minister Arthur Balfour formally opened Seaham's New South Dock on 11th November 1905. He was driven from Wynyard where he was the guest of the Londonderrys. At the ceremony Lord Londonderry pointed out the changes that had occurred at Seaham since the opening of the harbour. When Balfour addressed the crowd he said 'The prosperity of this region has gone on augmenting; that is one thing that has not, or if changed, at all events, has only changed for the better'. The Prime Minister then turned a handle on the quayside which started the hydraulic machinery which opened the inner dock gate. This was accompanied by cheering from the assembled crowd and whistles from the nearby steamers.

Arthur Balfour

NEW SOUTH DOCK, SEAHAM HARBOUR.

To mark the opening, the Seaham Harbour Dock Company held a dinner for 200 workers at the Castlereagh Hotel. The contractors S. Pearson & Son also held a dinner for 300 of their employees.

Left: The Castlereagh Hotel today is now called The Carlton.

Rhodes Visit

In May 1899 Cecil Rhodes stayed at Wynyard Park as the guest of the Marquess and Marchioness of Londonderry. He visited Seaham where he toured the Londonderry Railway Works, Docks, Conservative Club, Drill Hall and Nautical School.

Rhodes was one of the most influential men in Southern Africa. He had promoted British interests in the area in the previous decades to such an extent that he had a country named after him. At that time of his visit to Seaham, Rhodesia was part of the British Empire. Today that country is called Zimbabwe and is part of the Commonwealth.

Cecil Rhodes

Above: Seaham Hall Station early this century. This station was for the private use of the Londonderrys. Many of the family's important visitors used the station and avoided public gaze.

Left: The station today with a different exterior finish.

Wellington Remembered

The Duke of Wellington was a guest at Wynyard in 1827. His host, the 3rd Marquess of Londonderry, had served as Wellington's Adjutant-General during the Peninsula Campaign.

During his stay, Wellington travelled on the Seaham-Rainton rail line to see Londonderry's Rainton collieries.

The Duke also attended a public dinner held in his honour at the Exchange Building in Sunderland. On 4th October 1827 an estimated crowd of 40,000 lined the streets to get a glimpse of the 'Iron Duke'.

Duke of Wellington

The memory of Wellington's visit to Seaham lives on today in the public house that bears his name in South Railway Street.

Nationalisation

On the 1st January 1947 the old order was swept away with the nationalisation of the coal industry. There were great celebrations among the miners because they thought everything was going to be heaven. Safety became a much more important issue. Safety Officers were appointed, ours was Mr Scott and the Welfare Officer Mr Walker. The Seaham Collieries were part of No. 2 Area of the National Coal Board.

Joan Pace

ON THE HUSTINGS

*Early Parliamentarians ... MP in Lunatic Asylum ... Trouble at
Polls ... Honourable Members ... University of Seaham ...
Socialism defeats Communism ... Hero & Villain ... Gracie's
Message ... Towards the New Millennium*

John Cummings MP with Prime Minister
Tony Blair - occupants of two of the safest
parliamentary seats in the country.

Vanes and Tempests

Since the 1670s several members of the Vane and Tempest families served as MPs for Durham County. When the families joined through marriage and became the Vane Tempests this parliamentary tradition continued.

Frances Anne Vane Tempest married Charles William Stewart in 1819. Their son, Adolphus, was elected MP for Durham North.

Lord Adolphus Frederick Charles William Vane Tempest (Dolly to his family) served as MP for Durham North between 1854 and 1864. Towards the end of his parliamentary career his behaviour became increasingly bizarre as the incident reported in the *Seaham Observer* of 9th March 1861 shows *(right)*. The third son of the 3rd Marquess of Londonderry had served in the Crimean War with the Scots Guards and this could have been the cause of his later neurosis.

After his court appearance, Adolphus was transferred to a lunatic asylum and the charges against him dropped. He was to suffer bouts of madness until his death only three years later.

DRUNKEN FROLICS OF LORD ADOLPHUS VANE TEMPEST

On Wednesday, at the Marlborough street Police Court, London, Lord Adolphus Vane Tempest, M.P., was brought before Mr. Beadon, stipendiary magistrate, in custody of acting-inspector Silverton and P.C. Elliott, of the C. division, charged with disorderly conduct in Coventry street.

Defendant was brought to the court in a cab, and came before the magistrate with his dress in great disorder, having been carried upstairs by five or six officers. On being placed before the magistrate in a very excited state, he said: I suppose you know I am a member of the House of Commons?

Mr. Beadon, magistrate: I am not aware that you are.

Defendant: You are a liar.

Elliott: I found the gentleman in Coventry street, about four this afternoon.

Defendant here behaved himself in such a manner as to call from Mr. Beadon the remark: If you don't know how to behave yourself, I will wait till you do.

Elliott: I found him in the centre of the road stopping horses in the broughams and cabs that were passing. There was about 500 persons collected. I could not tell his object. The defendant was in a very excited state and very violent.

Defendant: Do you know I am a member of the House of Commons? Reporters put it down. I'll have it reported.

Elliott: He was throwing cigars about the crowd, and also his money. I then took him into custody. There was an obstruction of the public thoroughfare. The defendant was in the same excited state as now in the court, and there was great difficulty in getting him to the station.

Defendant: Did I strike you?

Elliott: No; you spat in my face.

Defendant, to the constable; are you a judge of numbers? Were there cigars and money enough for all the people.

Mr. Beadon, to defendant: Do you wish to say anything?

Defendant: Did I not say I was a member of the House of Commons? Don't you know (to the constable) that you have done an illegal thing? I ought to be at the House of Commons now. (Defendant stamped his feet on the table, having been accommodated with a chair.)

Other officers having stated that the defendant's conduct was exactly described by Elliott.

Mr. Beadon said: Will you give a reason for this conduct?

Defendant: I must be heard on oath then. Indeed, I have come here as a favour. I used to know Mr. Hardwick and Mr. Bingham, I was once fined 5s. (The defendant here began singing a tune from a popular opera, beating time on the front of the witness-box.)

Defendant (to the chief clerk who was writing): Now don't alter anything (again singing).

Mr. Beadon: It is perfectly clear that you are not at present responsible for your actions. I shall order you to find two sureties in £500 each to appear before me this day week.

Defendant (after whistling): Can't you take my bail for £1,000? Am I to go down stairs? You'll have to let me out again very soon.

The defendant was then removed from the court, after a scene seldom witnessed.

Polling Day Trouble

The General Election of 1874 resulted in serious disturbances in Seaham. By one o'clock in the afternoon of polling day on 9th February a large crowd had gathered in North Terrace. This was mostly comprised of Liberal-supporting miners, although probably none had been able to vote that day. The Second Reform Act passed seven years previously had only added skilled workers to the electorate. The total who could vote was still only two million (men only) out of a population of around 30 million.

The targets for the crowd's displeasure were those displaying red favours (at the time the colour of the Tories). The Conservative Committee Room in North Terrace had its windows broken. The Mill Inn at Seaham Colliery also had its windows smashed, its furniture broken and large quantities of spirits destroyed.

As darkness fell, the violence increased. The *Seaham Weekly News* reported: 'At this time the mob on the North Terrace could not number less than 3,000 persons, and was composed largely of Seaham Colliery miners, many from Murton Colliery, and some from Ryhope, labourers from the Chemical Works, and Bottlemakers; many women too were among the crowd, and some hundreds of half-grown lads.'

A wagon loaded with tar barrels was attacked and set on fire. The windows of shops came under a barrage of stones from the rampaging crowd. The forces of law and order could do little against such numbers. The police presence, despite receiving reinforcements during the day, only numbered seventeen.

A message was sent to Sunderland for military assistance. A detachment of soldiers arrived on the 9.30 train and this helped persuade the locals to make their way home.

Despite the Conservatives sweeping into power Durham North returned two Liberal MPs - Isaac Lowthian Bell and Charles Mark Palmer. However, this was

Although he owned collieries in Durham and Northumberland, Charles Mark Palmer is best remembered as the founder of Jarrow Shipbuilding Yard. He represented Durham North from 1874 until November 1885 when he became MP for Jarrow which he served until his death in 1907.

not the end of the matter. In May 1874 a Durham Court pronounced the election void on the grounds of intimidation. A new election was held the following month. The *Seaham Weekly News* threw its full weight behind the Conservative candidate George Elliott. It printed a full page supplement of Elliott's election meetings in the area. If this did not get the message across the paper printed details of exactly how to vote for the Conservative candidate *(below)*.

The new poll returned Elliott to Parliament along with the Liberal Palmer. A year later the unseated Bell was elected MP for Hartlepool.

North Durham Election.

How to Mark the Ballot Papers.

Electors who intend to support Sir George Elliot are informed that they must make a cross after his name on the ballot paper as shown below :—

Bell, Isaac Lowthian, The Hall, Washington, in the County of Durham, Esquire.	
ELLIOT, GEORGE, Houghton Hall, in County of Durham, Baronet.	**X**
Palmer, Charles Mark, Newcastle-on-Tyne, Esquire.	

Only one cross must be made, and that in the square on the right side of Sir George Elliot's name, which is second on the list between those of his two Radical opponents. Any other mark besides that of the cross, as shown above, will vitiate the ballot paper, and spoil the vote.

Honourable Members

During this century the constituents of Seaham have had an amazing array of national figures representing them in parliament.

Seaham's MP from 1922 until his retirement in 1929 was Sidney Webb. Sidney, along with his wife Beatrice, were leading figures in the early Labour Movement. They wrote *The History of Trade Unionism* (1894), started the journal *New Statesman* and founded the London School of Economics. At the 1922 General Election he gained 20,203 votes (59.9% of the poll). He retained his seat at the next two Elections with equal ease before standing down in 1929.

Sidney Webb's replacement as Seaham's Labour candidate in 1929 could not have had higher credentials - former Prime Minister Ramsay MacDonald.

University of Seaham

Beatrice Webb was a leading light of the Labour Party in her own right. When her husband became Seaham's MP she gave lectures, attended meetings and set up a circulating library of 200 books for the constituents. She encouraged local women to become involved in politics and sent a monthly news letter to the town's women. By the time of the 1923 Election, Beatrice could proudly declare 'there are always a group of women, sometimes 60 or 70, at the meetings. Last year if there were two or three one was agreeably surprised.'

These schemes to bring education to the people, Beatrice Webb dubbed the 'University of Seaham.'

Sidney and Beatrice Webb were regular visitors to Seaham in the '20s. In her diary Beatrice recalled how local miners' halls were put at their disposal for meetings at Elections. 'When the two other candidates apply for some hall, they (the miners' lodges) are far too honest to put up the price; but they solemnly reply that "when they know Mr Webb's dates they will let them have it for any other night," a reply which infuriates the Conservative and Liberal agents'.

Socialism defeats Communism

Communist leader Harry Pollitt contested the Seaham seat at the 1929 Election. The General Secretary of the Great Britain Communist Party from 1929 to 1956 trailed in 4th with 1,431 votes (2.9% of the poll). Pollitt was very much pro-Moscow and in the decade following his election defeat he supported Stalin's purges (which saw millions killed and imprisoned).

Right: Harry Pollitt at the headquarters of the Communist Party of Great Britain.

Hero & Villain

Within days of polling a massive 35,615 votes at Seaham in 1929, MacDonald became Prime Minister for a second time. The new Labour Government had to rely on the support of the Liberals at a time of economic crisis and soaring unemployment. After forming a National Government in August 1931 he called an Election in the October. At Seaham, MacDonald defeated an official Labour Party candidate in a close contest.

One of MacDonald's Election posters.

Ramsay MacDonald

Gracie's Message

Ramsay MacDonald had the support of one of the country's top entertainers in the 1935 Election. Gracie Fields was unable to campaign for him personally in Seaham but sent a message of support. The star sent a wire to MacDonald a week before the election:

Gracie Fields

Regret I am unable to come up to Seaham. Sailing for South Africa shortly and must finish my new picture by November 21st, a week later than yours.

Hope we will both be successful in our work and that we shall be able to sit back and say 'Thank heaven for the British public.'

Good luck, and may you, the best man, win.

Gracie Field's message of support was to no avail. Manny Shinwell (Labour) had more than double the votes of MacDonald (National Labour). Shinwell remained in Parliament for the next 35 years (for Easington from 1950).

Manny Shinwell

A large crowd gathered for the declaration of the result of the 1935 Seaham Election. Manny Shinwell then addressed the crowd: 'This great triumph is a vindication of the Labour Party during the past four years. In particular it is an indication that the miners and their wives and families have no further use for the man who betrayed the principles of the Labour Party.'

MacDonald did not wait for the declaration but returned to London on the sleeper. When he got off the train at King's Cross an attendant said he looked like a man who had just withstood a 20-round boxing contest.

Towards the Millennium

After the last war parliamentary boundaries were redrawn and Seaham became part of Houghton-le-Spring. By the time of the 1983 Election the town had become part of the Easington constituency.

In 1987, Labour's John Cummings became Easington MP when he gained 32,396 votes - 24,639 ahead of his nearest rival. In 1992 his majority increased and then in 1997 he had over thirty thousand more votes than Tory candidate Jason Hollands in second place.

After the declaration in 1997 John Cummings told party workers, 'Exciting times are ahead … I look forward to playing my part in this new Labour Government and bring forward policies to take us into the next century'.

Above: A poster from the 1997 Election campaign.

Left: John Cummings and Grit. Jack Russell terriers are one of the Easington MP's interests in his spare time.

After attending Murton Council Infants, Juniors and Seniors, he started as an apprentice electrician at Murton Colliery.

He served his political apprenticeship in the 1970s as an Easington District Councillor. He became Chairman in 1975 and was leader of the Council between 1979 and 1987 when he entered Parliament.

Local Government

Many well known residents served on Seaham Urban District Council over the years. Local shopkeepers, publicans, miners and businessmen all sought office. Before the elections of April 1919, prospective candidates published letters in the *Seaham Weekly News*. One of these was from timber importer Joseph Elgey who was seeking re-election:

Ladies and Gentlemen,

The day is fast approaching when my term of office as your representative will expire. I trust that my services have been of sufficient value to allow me to ask for your support at the forthcoming Election. I have had a long and varied experience in Municipal affairs, having been closely connected with all the important committees.

I am still the Independent Business Man who is willing to devote his time and experience for the benefit of his townspeople.

Should you choose to re-elect me I will carry out the duties to your satisfaction.

Yours sincerely,
JOSEPH ELGEY

Sawmills,
Seaham Harbour

Elgey was successfully returned in the Election, as was Henry Minski, auctioneer and house furnisher; J.W. Claxton, architect and surveyor; W. Moore, miner and J.W. Scott, manager of the Co-operative Society.

Some of the unsuccessful candidates included: William Hardy, landlord of the Bottlemakers' Arms; Thomas Dodds, landlord of the King's Arms and J. Warham, bank manager.

"THOR" (s.s.) 2,300 d.w., discharging props, crowntrees, chocks and deals in Seaham Harbour for J. ELGEY.

A trade card for Elgey's timber importing business early this century.

THIS SPORTING LIFE

Golf Club ... West Indian Star ... Footballing Tradition ... Red Star ... Seaham Lads ... Roker Park Treat ... Bullseye ... Wembley Excursions ... The Noble Art

A Seaham Harbour football card from March 1918 produced by J. Baines of Bradford. Baines were prolific producers of cards from the latter 1890s until the late 1920s when interest waned. They came in various shapes such as footballs, rugby balls, shields etc. They were sold in packets of 6 for $^1/_2$d for quite some time. In 1920 about 13 million cards were reported to have been sold, which was around their peak period. Even small towns and villages were included.

Right: The Seaham Golf Club House a few years after its construction. The club was set out on 95 acres of land given by the Londonderrys and opened for play on 15th May 1911.

Left: Golfers on the 1st Green at Seaham after the First World War. When the club first opened it had 173 men and 52 lady members. At the time the subscription fee was 2 guineas a year (men), 1 guinea (ladies) and 15 shillings (juniors under 18)

A tournament at Seaham Golf Club in 1997. The club is still going strong today with a waiting list for membership.

One of Seaham's cricket teams between the wars. Cricket has been one of the most popular and enduring of Seaham's pastimes.

The opening of the new ground of Seaham Harbour Cricket Club was due to take place on Whit Tuesday 1868. However, heavy rain caused the event to be cancelled. Instead of wasting the day, a match was played between married members of the club and single members. The bachelors won the game by four runs. Afterwards both sides retired to the Braddyll Arms for supper.

The ground adjoining Seaham Hall was eventually opened on 8th June 1868. Many of the one thousand people who gathered for the ceremony were ladies.

Right: An advert from the *Seaham Observer* for Seaham Harbour Cricket Club's new ground's original opening day.

SEAHAM CRICKET CLUB.
OPENING OF THE NEW GROUND.
A GRAND
GALA
WILL BE HELD IN THE
NEW CRICKET FIELD,
On WHIT-TUESDAY, June 2nd, 1868,
A HOME MATCH
Between 11 and 22 will be played, commencing at 11
THE SPLENDID
BAND OF THE 2ND DURHAM ARTIL-
LERY VOLUNTEERS
Will be in attendance and Play a Choice Selection
of Music during the Game.
DANCING
WILL COMMENCE ON THE GREEN AT FIVE O'CLOCK.
AUNT SALLY & OTHER GAMES.
TEA and other REFRESHMENTS will be Pro-
voided on the Ground on Moderate Terms.
Admission :—From 11 a.m. to 6.30 p.m., 6d ; after
6.30 p.m. 3d.

In the summer of 1932, West Indian Test bowler George Francis was Seaham Harbour's cricket professional. During the season the club paid out £364 on the professional's wages, talent money and travelling expenses. With regret the club did not engage Francis the following season because they could not meet his wage demands. Their funds had been depleted by the economic conditions in the district. Seaham Colliery had given notices to 350 men and Dawdon Colliery was working at well below capacity.

Seaham Harbour and Seaham Albion football clubs were founder members of the Wearside League in 1892-93. Seaham Harbour finished the season as champions. Albion also found early success, winning the Monkwearmouth Cup in 1899-90 and 1906-07. In 1900-01 season Seaham Thistle won the Hendon Junior Alliance. The following year they joined up with Seaham Villa, turning out as their 'A' team. But during the season the senior side disbanded and the youngsters fulfilled their fixtures. They went from strength to strength and joined the Wearside League in 1904-05. Another Seaham club - White Star, won the Wearside League in 1904-05 and 1907-08.

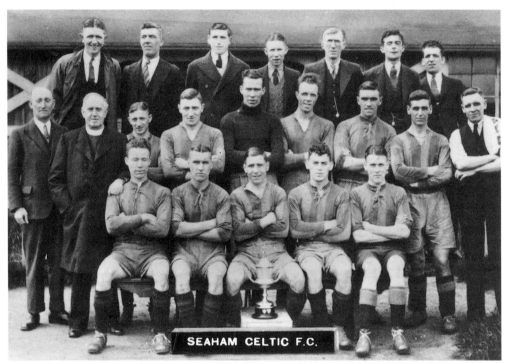

SEAHAM CELTIC F.C.

Seaham Celtic football team at the start of the 1935-36 season. The team changed its name from Seaham St Cuthbert's at the end of the 1934-35 season. In their last season as St Cuthbert's they won the Durham County Catholic Charity Cup.

They reached the Final by beating Easington Celtic 4-0. Their reward was an appearance at Roker Park against Washington

PHOTOCARDS

No. 54.
SEAHAM CELTIC F.C.

Left to right, back row :—*R. Parker (Committee), G. O'Connor (Committee), P. Lennon (Committee), E. Haggan, W. Elliott (Chairman), J. M'Donough (Treasurer), E. Bacon (Committee).* Second row :—*W. Wallace (Secretary), Rev. Fr. M. J. Haggarty (President), F. Brace, H. Brace (Capt.), J. Elliott, A. Givens, D. Sharvin, R. Brown, O. Garrigan (Trainer).* Front row:— *O. Haggan, J. O'Connor, T. Elliott, T. Clark, B. McQuillan.* This club, previously known as Seaham St. Cuthberts, are members of the Seaham and District League, and in season 1984/35, they had the distinction of winning the Durham County Catholic Charity Cup the final of which was played at Roker Park.

ARDATH TOBACCO CO. LTD. Manufacturers of STATE EXPRESS and ARDATH CIGARETTES

St Joseph's. In a close first half the sides were deadlocked at 1-1. After the interval St Cuthbert's scored twice to secure a famous victory.

New Seaham boys football team in the 1907-08 season when they played in the Sunderland Schools' League.

Seaham Red Star 1996-97 season: Back row (left to right) Alan Farquar, Graeme Mole, Mark Riches, Alan Pearson, Kevin Stevens, Anthony Howarth. Front row (left to right) Mark Gallagher, Lee Graham, Rob Ferguson, Steve Smith (captain), Peter Ould, Tom Cruickshanks.

Seaham Lads

Many Seaham footballers have gone on to play the game professionally, some with neighbouring Sunderland and others farther afield.

One of Sunderland's greatest footballers before the First World War was Seaham's George Holley. In November 1904 George joined Sunderland from Seaham White Star. He had only made a dozen appearances for White Star but had a record of better than a goal per game. He had started his football as a 14-year-old with Seaham Young Villa before moving to Seaham Athletic, Seaham Villa and then White Star. The brilliant inside left went on to score more than 150 League and Cup goals for Sunderland and won 10 England caps. Teammate Charlie Buchan recalled how one day, when picking up his wage packet, manager Bob Kyle asked 'Do you think you've earned it?' He replied 'No, but I think George has earned it for all of us.'

Another Seaham White Star player to go on to the professional ranks was Levi Thorpe. During his White Star

GEO. HOLLEY, SUNDERLAND A.F.C

When he joined Sunderland in 1904 George Holley received 30 shillings a week. Some of today's players are on £50,000 a week.

days he lived with his parents at 47 Stewart Street, New Seaham. In 1911, he left his job as a miner to join Blackpool. The right half later played for Burnley, Blackburn Rovers and Rochdale.

Although born at a hospital in Sunderland, Gary Rowell is a Seaham lad. One of Sunderland's all-time favourites, only a serious injury stopped Gary breaking the club's post-war goalscoring record. The highlight of his career was his hat-trick in the 4-1 victory against Newcastle at St James' Park in 1979. The classy striker was also one of the coolest penalty-takers ever to wear the red and stripes.

One of the heroes of Sunderland's 1973 triumph, Ritchie Pitt, played for Seaham Boys in the '60s. An England

Gary Rowell, one of Sunderland's greatest post-war players.

Schoolboy international, the highlight of the centre half's Seaham career was an English Schools' Trophy semi-final at Roker Park. Seaham were by far the better team in the game against Liverpool but went down 3-2.

Seaham-born Brian Marwood played League football for Arsenal, Hull City, Middlesbrough (loan) and both Sheffield clubs. Milestones in Brian's career included: a League championship with Arsenal in 1988-89, a full England cap and chairmanship of the Professional Footballers' Association.

Another Seaham sportsman had an important influence on Brian's decision to become a footballer. England cricketer Peter Willey advised against becoming a professional cricketer on financial grounds. Brian turned his back on a cricket career with Northants to become a footballer.

The title of most-capped Seaham footballer must go to Terry Fenwick. He turned out no less then twenty times for England, including the 1986 World Cup where he faced Maradona & co. Terry played almost all his League football in London, turning out for Crystal Palace, Queens Park

Ritchie Pitt, Seaham and Sunderland

Rangers and Spurs. He was always the first name Terry Venables would put on the team sheet.

Tough centre half John Wile was on Sunderland's books in the '60s but made his name at West Bromwich Albion.

In more recent times, Seaham Red Star's Nigel Gleghorn made the step up to League football with Ipswich Town and later played for Manchester City and Birmingham City.

Brian Marwood (standing right) of the Professional Footballers' Association with young players at a Durham County Schools' Festival at Houghall College in Durham. Brian is now one of the top men at the sports company Nike.

Paul Nixon played for Seaham Boys and County Durham Boys in the mid '70s. After moving to New Zealand, Paul was selected for the full New Zealand international team (the All Whites). On returning to this country for a holiday he was signed by Gerry Francis for Bristol Rovers. The highlights of his Rovers' career were winning the Third Division Championship and playing at Wembley in the

Paul Nixon

Leyland-Daf Cup Final. Paul, who is the brother-in-law of England cap Brian Marwood, is now back in New Zealand where he runs a business.

Frank Reed played in goal for Camden Square School and Sunderland Boys. My wife's grandfather, Anthony Seed, was brother of Jimmy Seed, the Charlton manager. He was responsible for many North East players going to Charlton, including Sam Bartram. I did not meet him until some years after Frank went to Charlton, but when I mentioned I knew Frank from my Seaham days,

Frank Reed

he told me he had recommended Frank to Charlton. Frank went on to play in the first team.

George Hoare

Bullseye

In 1937 Seaham Darts League was one of the largest in the county with 500 members. That season's champs were Ryhope's Queen's Head Inn (*below*).

SEAHAM DARTS LEAGUE TABLE TO DATE

FINAL TABLE

	P	W	L	D	F	A	Pts.
1. Queen's Head Inn	38	27	7	4	189	115	58
† Braddyll Arms	38	23	6	9	178	126	55
† Railway Inn	38	25	9	4	189	115	54
4. Engineer's Arms	38	24	8	6	186	118	54
5. Castlereagh Hotel	38	21	7	10	180	124	52
6. Oddfellows Arms	38	18	6	14	175	129	50
7. Times Inn	37	12	9	16	152	144	40
8. Station Hotel	38	15	8	154	150	38	
9. New Seaham Inn	38	12	13	13	155	149	37
10. Irish Club	37	11	11	15	136	160	37
11. Mill Inn	38	10	14	14	146	158	34
12. Edinbrugh Castle	38	10	16	12	143	161	32
13. Duke of Wellington	38	14	20	4	142	162	32
14. King's Arms	38	9	15	14	139	165	32
15. R.A.O.B.	38	10	17	11	133	171	31
16. Toll Bar	38	10	21	7	129	175	27
17. Volunteer Arms	38	11	23	4	132	172	26
18. Londonderry Arms	38	9	22	7	168	176	25
19. Vane Arms	38	8	24	6	126	178	22
20. Guide Post	38	6	22	10	123	181	22

† Inquiry pending.

Cycle Parade

At the turn of the century cycling was a popular pastime in the area. Seaham Benevolent Cycling Club used to hold an annual church service and parade. On Sunday 28th August 1904 this was held in the grounds of Seaham Hall. More than 1,200 cyclists gathered on North Terrace Green and, preceded by a brass band, made their way to the Hall. Cycling clubs from Houghton, Washington, Chester-le-Street, Sunderland, Shotton and Ferryhill all attended. New Seaham had 100 members alone with lady cyclists well represented.

A coach trip leaving Seaham for the 1932 FA Cup Final. For those wishing to make the trip by rail there was an LNER excursion which left Seaham at 10.19 pm on Friday. For the fare of 19/6d you could spend the morning in London then a train would take you from Marylebone to Wembley.

Before the war, there used to be regular trips to Finals. Unlike today, getting tickets for the game was no problem.

Roker Park Treat

My dad used to take me to the matches at Roker Park in the 1930s. We used to get the autocar from Seaham Station to Sunderland. I suppose it was something like today's Metro. We would then get a tram from outside the Museum to the top of Gladstone Street and walk to the ground.

In the pre-war years, hundreds of supporters would go to matches from Seaham. They walked, cycled, travelled by bus or train to watch their beloved Sunderland. They had a great team at this time and

George Forster, with son Robert and daughter Mandy, sitting on the steps at the Roker End of Roker Park in 1971.

there were always big crowds. For part of the game I would be on my dad's shoulders but when he got tired I had to stand. This was a nightmare, because all I'd see were the backs of people and could only listen to the 'oohs and aahs', clapping and cheering. The youngsters of today don't have this problem as the Stadium of Light offers great views for everybody.

George Forster

The Noble Art

The 'Fighting Devlins' are the most famous boxing family Dawdon has ever produced. Brothers Tommy, Billy, Andy, Jimmy, Terry and Gene all combined work at Dawdon Colliery with careers in the ring. They got their love of the fight game from their father Bill, who always used to know what presents to buy his sons - boxing gloves. The Devlins were never short of local support in their bouts before and after the war.

A man who fought no less than three of the Devlin brothers was another Dawdon favourite - Tommy Ray. Ray drew with Tommy Devlin in a 10 round bout at Seaham Harbour in September 1927. Nine years later he fought Billy and Andy Devlin within a month of each other, with Ray winning both contests, again at Seaham Harbour.

In the early part of this century, Seaham Colliery-born Billy Hughes was one of the finest bantamweights in the country. In an unofficial world title fight he took Digger Stanley to the 17th round before suffering defeat. Stanley went on to claim a version of the world championship while Hughes had to settle for the title of 'pitmen's champion'.

Between the wars fights were staged at Billy Hughes' Seaham Harbour Physical Culture Grounds. The fight card of 13th August 1932 drew in over 2,000 spectators. Andy Devlin made short work of Tom Davison (Seaham Colliery) when the referee stopped the fight in the 3rd. Tommy Ray was beaten by Cyclone Billy Evans (Canada) on points over 8 rounds. Billy Sinclair (Murton) knocked out Eddie Turnbull (Stockton) in the 4th of a scheduled 6 rounder. Dick Bartlett (Seaham Harbour) faced Tom Powell (Stockton) the cruiserweight champion of India. Powell claimed the purse and side stake of £75 after an injury to Bartlett's eye forced his retirement in the 4th round.

Today Seaham Leisure Centre stages professional boxing bills. On 13th February 1998 the arena staged a British Lightweight eliminator between Hartlepool's Alan Temple and Bradford's Bobby Vanzie. The Yorkshireman proved too strong, knocking Temple out in the third round before a capacity crowd at Seaham.

Other bouts on the Gus Robinson promotion saw Peter Mason (Blackhall) beat Paul Bonson (Featherstone) on points and John Green (Middlesbrough) defeat Hughie Davey (Wallsend) also on points.

World Record

In the '20s Seaham could claim its very own world record-holder. Dawdon miner George Davison punched a ball continuously for over 60 hours to put himself in the record books.

He started his attempt at 10.20 am on Wednesday 15th September 1926 at Seaham Harbour School of Physical Culture. Sustained by a diet of bananas, biscuits, eggs and meat, the 35-year-old former soldier passed the old mark of 60 hours on the Saturday morning. This was greeted by a huge roar from his many supporters. He continued for a further two hours and then finished with a flourish by knocking the ball of the hook with his last punch.

From a Jack to a Gene

Gene Devlin, one of the famous Dawdon boxing family, got his name via an unusual route. He was born on the day of a world heavyweight title fight between Jack Dempsey and Gene Tunney. Mr Devlin said he would name his son after the winner of the bout. As Dempsey was expected to win the odds were on the name Jack but Tunney won and Gene it was to be.

AT THE BAR

*Good Stabling at the Mill Inn ... Lord Seaham ... From
Londonderry to Sylvia's ... Adam & Eve ... Time Gentleman
Please ... Vane Arms ... The Phoenix rises from the ashes of the
Seaton Colliery Inn ... Edinburgh Castle ... Paddy Finn's*

The Kestrel on Station Road in 1998. Public houses went up alongside the
growing town of Seaham. Of the ten pubs listed in *Pigot's Directory* of 1834:
Golden Lion, King's Arms, Londonderry Arms, Lord Seaham, Lynn Arms,
Masons' Arms, Noah's Ark, Wellington, Wheatsheaf, Windmill, half have
survived, some under new names.

The Mill Inn of today dates from 1892 but this had replaced an older inn on the site. This had taken its name from an old mill (Nicky Nack House) that stood nearby.

Horsemen, Cyclists & Motorists

Before the First World War Daniel Anderson was proprietor of the Mill Inn at New Seaham. His establishment boasted 'Good stabling and accommodation for cyclists. Motor spirit kept in stock.'

Ward's Directory 1899-1900

William Edward Chadwick	Noah's Ark hotel, 1 North Railway Street
Robert Chorley	Northumberland Arms hotel, 27 South Railway Street
James Deuchar Ltd	Forresters' Arms inn, 10 North Railway Street
Patrick Finn	Bottle Makers' Arms inn, 10 Pilot Terrace
Adam C. Harrison	Golden Lion inn, South Railway Street
George Alex Hope	Ship inn, 5 North Railway Street
William McKenna	Kings' Arms hotel, 9 North Terrace
Thomas Nasbet jun.	Station hotel, 40 Marlborough Street
Fred Palmer	Lord Seaham hotel, North Terrace
George Pollard	Highlander inn, Back North Terrace
Alfred Reynolds	Vane Arms inn, 74 Church Street
Isaac Saville	Duke of Wellington hotel, 8 South Railway Street
William F. Smith	Braddyll Arms inn, Adolphus Street
Johnson Russell Thompson	Rose & Crown inn, 13 Church Street
Samuel Paterson Thompson	Castlereagh hotel, Castlereagh Road
Henry Michael Walker	Londonderry Arms inn, 4 South Crescent

As well as public houses the Directory also lists beer retailers (as opposed to full licence holders). These included: Edinburgh Castle, Zetland Hotel, Canterbury Arms, Engineers' Arms, Volunteer Arms, Blandford Arms and Dene Cottage in Adam and Eve Gardens.

The Lord Seaham Inn, North Terrace in the middle of the last century.

The completion of the rail line from Rainton allowed coal to be shipped from Seaham in huge quantities. The brig *Lord Seaham* was the first ship loaded at Seaham after the official opening of the dock on 25th July 1831. Owned by the Marquess of Londonderry, the *Lord Seaham,* after taking on board 300 tons of coal, was towed out of harbour amidst great celebration. Crowds cheered, cannons were fired, while off shore crowded vessels from Sunderland and Hartlepool looked on.

The Lord Seaham Hotel is still in business today and is now known as the Harbour View.

The first house to be built in Seaham Harbour was The Londonderry Arms public house. The foundation stone of the building was laid in 1828 and the pub is still going strong after 170 years.

The Londonderry is now called Sylvia's but the old style bar is one of the features that has not changed today.

The late Sylvia Goodlass with pet python Molly in 1978, when the pub was still known as the Londonderry Arms. The pub is now called Sylvia's in the landlady's honour.

A short distance along South Terrace from Sylvia's is the Engineers Arms. This old pub has served workers in the harbour and docks and visiting seamen since the last century.

The Adam and Eve Gardens were founded in the 1830s by Ralph Fair. From their earliest days they were popular with the residents of the growing new town of Seaham Harbour.

At the Licensing Sessions in 1931, Frank Marriott, licence holder of the Dene Cottage Inn, Adam and Eve Gardens, applied for the transfer of the licence to a new pub to be built near Seaham Station. The owners, J. Nimmo & Son of Castle Eden, said in addition, they were also willing to give up the licence of the Marlborough House, North Terrace, if the transfer was agreed.

The out door tables for customers are reminiscent of modern pubs but this is an old picture of the pub in the Adam and Eve Gardens.

After the pub closed the Adam and Eve Gardens were still run as a market garden. *Above:* The site of the Adam and Eve Gardens today.

Time Gentleman Please

In May 1906 Thomas Scully, landlord of the Canterbury Arms, North Railway Street, appeared at Seaham Police Court. He was charged with being open during prohibited hours on Sunday. The court heard from two police officers who had entered the pub on a Sunday afternoon at 3.15 and found the accused, his wife and seven German sailors all with drinks in front of them. The landlord told the court the sailors were from a steamer in the docks and the front door of the pub had been accidentally left open. This was to allow people to leave not enter the pub. The Bench thought Scully was close to breaking the law but accepted his explanation and dismissed the case.

The Vane Arms in Church Street early this century

The Oddfellows Arms is the last
surviving pub in Church Street today.

The Volunteer Arms has Frances
Street all to itself today.

The Inn Between in South Railway Street was formerly called the Northumberland Arms. At the time of going to press, owner Billy Walker, hopes to get permission to revert back to the pub's old name.

Boarded up and for sale, Lorimers in Blandford Place early in 1998. This pub was formerly called The Blandford.

Left: Time is called on another Seaham public house: The Edinburgh Castle in the process of demolition.

Bar staff and customers outside the Seaton Colliery Inn in the 1890s. In an air-raid on the night of 21st October 1941, a bomb completely destroyed the pub. The landlord's wife was killed along with another woman and a further dozen people were injured.

In the '50s a new pub was built to replace the Seaton Colliery Inn. Appropriately, for this rebuilding from the ashes of the bombed pub, the new name was The Phoenix.

Behind the bar at the Seaton Colliery Inn at the time of the First World War. Note that Bovril was one of the beverages on offer at the inn.

The bar of The Phoenix today still retains an old fashion pub atmosphere. Present landlord Adrian Marshall has been at the Phoenix for fifteen years. In that time Adrian and his regulars have raised thousands of pounds for a variety of charities.

Station Hotel

The Station Hotel closed its doors for the last time on 9th September 1968. It had been built in the middle of the last century at the Seaham Harbour terminus of the railway link to Hendon. George Keegan was the last landlord of the Station Hotel. However, at the time of its closure it was still known by locals as 'Paddy Finn's' after a turn of the century landlord.

The Golden Lion used to stand next to the Theatre Royal. At one time both establishments had the same proprietor - Mr Adam C. Harrison.

Dempsey's Bar

Seaham's newest pub, Dempsey's Bar in North Terrace, is named after heavyweight boxing champion of the '20s, Jack Dempsey. Formerly Cassandra's restaurant, owners Stan and Ann Goodings converted the building to a bar in 1997. The couple used to be mine hosts at the Noah's Ark.

After retiring from boxing the 'Manassa Mauler' ran his own bar in New York for many years and his was called 'Jack Dempsey's.'

SECTION NINE

ON THE BEACH

Beer Galore ... Featherbed Rocks ... South Beach ... Butter Galore ... Guns on the Beach ... The Day We Nearly Lost The Lighthouse ... German Submarine ... Fishing ... Gardeners' Delight

The Featherbed Rock and North Beach.

Beer Galore

The steamer *General Havelock* went aground off Hendon on the night of 27th September 1894. All but one of its passengers and crew got off safely before the vessel began to break up. Two days later the beach at Seaham was covered in stores from the wreck. Local children picked up large quantities of apples and pomegranates. Chests of tea, barrels of vinegar and packages of candles were also washed ashore.

A barrel of beer landed near the Featherbed Rock. A coastguardsman took charge of the barrel but a group of men forcibly took possession of it. They broke it open and used hands, hats and even boots to drink from it. The more organised took the beer away in buckets. Some of those who stayed became so drunk they lay on the beach unable to stand. The coastguard had to rescue several from the advancing surf or they would have drowned. A couple of weeks later nine men appeared at Seaham Harbour Petty Sessions. They were found guilty of drunkenness on the beach and were fined.

Seaham Harbour from the North.

Featherbed Rock and beach in 1858. Earlier that century Byron, during his stay at Seaham, used to enjoy scrambling up Featherbed Rock with his wife.

The Featherbed Rock has suffered the same fate – erosion by the elements and then collapse – as its neighbour up the coast at Marsden.

South Beach with the Bottleworks on the cliff top. The Bottleworks were opened by John Candlish in 1853 and continued to grow until bottles made in Seaham were exported all over the world. The works closed down in 1921 and were finally demolished in 1950.

Youngsters plodge in the surf on the North Beach between the wars. A few of the more intrepid inhabitants of Seaham would brave the cold North Sea for a swim.

Butter Galore

The scenes on Seaham beach in the early days of 1899 must have been reminiscent of something from Compton MacKenzie's *Whisky Galore*.

On New year's Eve 1898 the Tyneside-bound steamer *Niord* went aground on rocks off Seaham in thick fog. A boat from the ship made it ashore and then the lifeboat took off the captain and the rest of the crew. The ship began to break up and some of her cargo washed ashore.

The *Niord* was carrying a cargo of 2,504 casks of butter, 161 bales of bacon and 80 cases of eggs. On 2nd January thousands of people were on the beach helping themselves to butter and bacon (it appears the eggs did not survive the rough seas). The police were powerless to stop the goods being carried away. The following day reinforcements arrived and arrests were made.

A few days later at Seaham Harbour Petty Sessions 28 people were convicted of larceny of butter and bacon. Most thought they were doing nothing wrong when taking the salvaged goods. The quantities varied, one man was found guilty of taking 58 lbs of bacon. Most of the fines ranged from 2/6 to 5 shillings. The severest punishment was reserved for two Sunderland men who were caught taking 30 lbs of butter but resisted arrest and had to be handcuffed. The 'out of towners' were fined 20 shillings and costs.

Casks of butter washed ashore from the *Niord* soon attracted the attention of locals and then the police.

The North Battery-Seaham

The gun battery on the North Beach in the last century. The four guns were manned by members of Seaham Volunteers.

Sea Banks, Seaham Harbour

By the turn of the century the guns had gone but the emplacements survived until the 1930s when they were washed away in a storm.

Bessy's Hole, Seaham Harbour. 5520

Above: Bessy's Hole was the north east boundary between Dalton-le-Dale and the old parish of Seaham.

Below: The old Baths and Coastguard Station. The point where the Dene met the sea was filled in to build the coast road. *Right:* The view today.

The Day We Nearly Lost The Lighthouse

Around 1960, a few of us were on holiday in Devon. Staying at the same place was an ex-army Captain. He was very friendly and regaled us with tales of his army days. Most of his anecdotes began 'when I was in the Khyber Pass', but in conversation it transpired he had been stationed at Seaham during the war.

He recounted how he arrived at Seaham Station in the middle of the night, when everything was pitch dark because of the black-out. He needed to be at the Docks where he was to be accommodated on board ship. Enquiring of directions, he was told the simplest way was to follow the mineral line which ran down to the Docks. He was warned to always keep the line to a certain side of him, although he could not recall which. Stumbling along in the dark was not easy and he soon became fed up. Hearing voices he called in the general direction of the sound and was asked to identify himself. Completely forgetting earlier instructions he moved in the direction of the voice, calling out 'Capt - a - i - n', which was as far as he got when he found no ground beneath his feet and, very quickly, a dirty coal-hold. Having been helped out of his predicament a rather dishevelled Captain finally arrived at his destination.

The Beach, Seaham Harbour. (5813)

The old lighthouse was demolished in the last war because it was in the line of fire of the defence guns. But the new lighthouse almost suffered the same fate.

A few days later, clean and recovered, he thought it time to inspect the gun under his command housed on the cliff-tops. First impressions left him doubtful as to the safety of the dug-out. Going into the dug-out increased his doubts. Attaching a lanyard to the gun, he moved outside before firing. His fears proved to be well-founded as the whole structure collapsed. He gave instructions to re-build the structure and make sure the gun was completely camouflaged. When this was done to his satisfaction he decided to have target-practice. Out to sea went a boat towing the target. Taking readings, the Captain gave instructions to the gunner then gave the order to fire. To his surprise the shell narrowly missed the new lighthouse and the target by a long way. After re-checking his readings, the Captain issued fresh instructions, as by now the boat and target had travelled some distance, and gave the order to fire. This time, the shell whistled past the other side of the lighthouse and the target by some distance, yet again. Thoroughly perplexed, the Captain checked round the outside and noticed something shining amongst the camouflage, which turned out to be the end of the gun. Demanding an explanation, he was told when the camouflage ran out a small portion of the barrel was still protruding so the end was sawn off in order to hide it!

The final outcome was not known to our Captain as he was given another posting shortly after.

George Hoare

The Beach, Seaham.

A crowded beach scene in front of the Featherbed Rock early this century. The beach was a playground for generation after generation of Seaham folk. During the First World War, a German submarine surfaced a few hundred yards off the beach and fired thirty shells at the town. Most missed their target but one lady was killed when a shell exploded in the colliery yard.

Today the Featherbed Rock has gone and so have the people.

Crowds pack the beach before the war. During the last war the beach was closed to the public. Sections of barbed wire were erected in case of an enemy beach landing.

Right: After the war a promenade was built at a cost of £168,000. *Below:* The same scene today.

THE PROMENADE, SEAHAM

Two anglers, wrapped up well against the elements, take a break on the pier. Fishing is one of the most popular participation sports in Seaham.

Gardeners' Delight

In May 1935 around a thousand bamboo canes were washed ashore on a half mile stretch of beach at Seaham. Word soon got around of the bounty and gardeners rushed down to claim them for use as pea sticks. It was thought the canes came from a ship unloading fruit and vegetables in a Dutch port.

SECTION TEN

HARD TIMES

Workers vs Masters ... Soup Kitchens ... On the Streets, Almost ...
Helping the Poor Bairns ... Emigration ... The Summer of '26 ...
Peril of the Sea ... The Lifeboat Disaster ... Deadly Diseases

Raging seas engulf the pier. Storms off the Seaham coast have claimed many lives over the years.

Workers vs Masters

From early in the last century Durham mining unions fought for the welfare and rights of their members. In 1831 Tommy Hepburn led a successful strike of Durham and Northumberland miners. In 1844 the region's miners were in dispute again with 33,990 Durham men on strike. A propaganda war was waged with the publication of broadsheets by both sides. Lord Londonderry tried to intimidate those in Seaham who tried to help the strikers who worked in mines outside of town. He published what became known as the *Seaham Letter*:

Lord Londonderry again warns all the shopkeepers and tradesmen in his town of Seaham that if they still give credit to pitmen who hold off work, and continue in the Union, such men will be marked by his agents and overmen, and will never be employed in his collieries again, and the shopkeepers may be assured that they will never have any custom or dealings with them from Lord Londonderry's large concerns that he can in any manner prevent.

Lord Londonderry further informs the traders and shopkeepers, that having by his measures increased very largely the last year's trade to Seaham, and if credit is so improperly and so fatally given to his unreasonable pitmen, thereby prolonging the injurious strike, it is his firm determination to carry back all the outlay of his concerns even to Newcastle.

Because it is neither fair, just or equitable that the resident traders in his own town should combine, and assist the infatuated workmen and pitmen in prolonging their own miseries by continuing an insane strike, and an unjust and senseless warfare against their proprietors and masters.

Londonderry and other coalowners imported blacklegs from as far away as Ireland and Wales to break the strike. To make way for these men, thousands of miners and their families were evicted from their homes. In August 1844 the strikers were forced to concede defeat and return to work.

The monument to the 6th Marquess of Londonderry on North Terrace.

Londonderry's Paternalism

The Londonderrys ran various schemes to help the poor over the years. These included the Poor People's Christmas Dinner Fund, Boot Fund and the Needle Work Guild.

The 6th Marquess and local businessmen annually raised money to give the poor a Christmas Dinner.

In 1904 this enabled 350 of Seaham's poor to be given some seasonal cheer. The head of each family was given a voucher for 1 lb of beef, a loaf of bread and half a stone of potatoes: large families were given double vouchers.

When the 6th Marquess died in 1915 his family erected a monument to him outside the Londonderry Offices. The inscription reads: 'This statue is placed here by his son and his daughter amongst those whom he loved so well and whose welfare and happiness were to him the principal objects of his life'.

In 1926 a total of £44 4s 6d was raised by subscription for the Poor People's Christmas Dinner Fund. This bought beef, vegetables, bread, tea and sweets for 250 of Seaham Harbour's poor. The people were again not given the money to buy the goods themselves but given vouchers for local shops.

At this time there was also a Seaham Harbour Boot Fund with Lord Londonderry donating £50. At the turn of the century Lady Londonderry's Needle Work Guild provided winter clothing for the poor.

Soup Kitchens

The hard winter of 1860-61 brought severe hardship to many people in Seaham. The struggle to provide food for the table was compounded by the need to buy coal to keep warm. When families had pawned everything they had they could appeal to the Board of Guardians for a two shillings payment but this was only given for one week.

In January 1861 a meeting was held at the Londonderry Literary Institute to discuss the distress in the town. The outcome was the setting up of a soup kitchen. A subscription raised £37 3s 6d. A £5 donation from Frances Anne, Marchioness of Londonderry, led the way followed by Earl Vane and the local clergy. The owners of South Hetton Colliery provided 30 tons of coal for distribution.

The Seaham Harbour soup kitchen opened on the 17th January and served 250 pints of soup to 140 people.

Breakfast on Minski

At Christmas 1904 Henry Minski gave a free breakfast for 250 poor children. They were entertained at the Londonderry Cafe in Seaham Harbour. The children were given tea, coffee, buns and cakes. Anything they could not eat they were allowed to take home.

Right: An advertisement for Henry Minski's at the time of his free breakfast for poor children. Another of Minski's enterprises was a pawnbroker's business. This provided a lifeline to poor families to help them over periods of cash crisis.

On the Streets, Almost

When my grandfather died in 1917, my grandmother was left to bring up her five children alone and was going to be put out of their colliery house. She went to the colliery manager and explained her predicament but got no joy and was told she would have to get out. 'What have I to do with the children?' she asked. My grandmother then said 'I'll tell you what, I'll go away and drown the lot of them'. The amused colliery manager said 'Oh don't take such drastic action' and he got her a job as caretaker at the High Colliery school next to the house. My mother qualified as a teacher and in 1917 started working at the school where grandmother was caretaker.

Joan Pace

Thinking of Others

Not all fund raising events were aimed at helping the needy of Seaham. A young Seaham Harbour girl called Ida Wilson used to organize bazaars in her parents house in North Terrace to help the poor children of Sunderland. In December 1909, when aged just 11, she raised £2 6s 6d for the Mayor's Fund. This was not the first time the youngster had contributed to the Fund, the first year she raised 10s 6d and the second year £2 1s 6d.

General Booth

Salvation Army founder General William Booth made a fleeting visit to Seaham on 28th August 1905. He called at the town on a motor tour of the country. He did have time to address a meeting at the Theatre Royal. One of the topics covered was emigration. Booth had set out his ideas in a book published in 1890 called *In Darkest England and the Way Out*. This proposed for those in social distress the formation of self-sustaining communities along the lines of the Co-operative society. There would be three types: the City Colony, the Farm Colony and the Over-Sea Colony. He believed the Salvation Army was destined to solve the problem of getting people back to the land and ultimately these would make a fresh start overseas.

At Seaham, Booth revealed that 3,500 people had been sent out to Canada. He declared 'Not a man or woman was selected for whom work could not be found. Of the thousand emigrants sent out in one vessel last year not one was without a situation when the boat arrived.'

General William Booth

A call for Seaham folk to emigrate to America or the four corners of the Empire just before the First World War. For some this was an opportunity to make a fresh start in a new country.

Seaham's Empire Theatre staged a film lecture 'The Great Land of Canada' on 8th March 1929. Major W.H. Hay of the Canadian Pacific Railway appealed to those with a pioneer spirit amongst those in the crowded theatre 'If a man worked from five to seven years and saved £100, the Government would advance him £500 to buy a farm of his own'.

The opportunity to start a new life in Canada was supported by G.R. Smith the acting manager of the Seaham Harbour Branch Employment Exchange. The local Council appealed to the town's unemployed to give migration consideration. A number of enquiries were made afterwards and application forms handed out.

An advert from the Seaham Weekly News from November 1890 for cheap passage to the United States and Canada.

A chance for local miners to work in Pennsylvania from the Seaham Observer in August 1869.

New Zealand Boys

Between the wars the New Zealand Sheep Owners ran a migration scheme. This allowed boys of officers and men of the Royal Navy, Merchant Marine and Fisherman, who had died or were disabled in the First World War, to migrate to the other side of the world. Seaham Harbour Employment Exchange supported the scheme and the kit issued to the boys was on display in a shop in Lord Street in February 1931.

In Good Health

In autumn 1926 Beatrice Webb visited Seaham with her husband. In her diary she noted one of the welcome consequences of the strike was an improvement in the health of the miners and their families.

She commented:

The surface facts show no exceptional distress: indeed the pit villages look clean and prosperous and the inhabitants healthy (death rate unusually low). Various people told us that the men and boys had benefited by the rest, sun, and open air and abstinence from alcohol and tobacco ... And the women freed from coal dust and enjoying regular hours; whilst the school-children, through the ample supply of first-class food (eleven meals each week at a cost of 3/6 per child at wholesale prices) were certainly improved in health and happiness. The one want was clothing and boots, and our gift of £100 to the Repair Fund was much appreciated.

The Summer of '26

My mother told me that during the 1926 strike wives of strikers would take their children to the parks and tennis courts. They would take with them home-made jam and bread and have picnics. It was a glorious summer.

Joan Pace

Prize Fighting

During the 1926 Strike boxing competitions were held with the winner taking away a bag of groceries. The victor had to beat as many as four men to claim his prize.

Dawdon Workmen's Club, like most of the local community, rallied round to support the striking miners and their families. Feeding stations like this one helped the miners stay out all summer.

Men at Seaham Colliery during the 1926 Strike. At the back, left, is Benny Hodges who was cashier but had to help in the mine to maintain the safety of the colliery whilst the miners were on strike.

The 1984-85 Strike was another long bitter battle for Seaham's miners. As in 1926, women played an important part in getting their families through the struggle. The outcome was also similar to that of sixty years before: the men were forced back to work. The strike had been fought over pit closures and by 1992 all three Seaham Collieries had closed.

One enterprising local businessman found the strike provided an opportunity for one of his products. This advert appeared in the *Seaham Weekly News* in October 1926.

On the March

In January 1934 the future Jarrow MP Ellen Wilkinson led a delegation of 300 people from Hebburn, Felling and Jarrow to see Prime Minister Ramsay MacDonald at Seaham. They were protesting at the treatment of the unemployed. They travelled part of the journey by train but then walked the last nine miles with a gale blowing in their faces. MacDonald saw Ellen Wilkinson but she was unimpressed with what he had to say. However, they were heartened by the welcome from Seaham folk as Ellen recalled in her autobiography *The Town That Was Murdered*: 'We got back to where the blessed women of Seaham Harbour Labour Party had provided hot tea and pies for the marchers.'

The incident brought Jarrow to the attention of the national press. Two years later the unemployed of the Tyneside town were to make a much more famous march to London - The Jarrow Crusade.

The lifeboat-house at Seaham Harbour earlier this century. Between 1870 and 1979 the town's lifeboats saved almost 300 lives.

A massive wave soars higher than the lighthouse in a storm in January 1998. Raging seas off Seaham in 1961 were responsible for the lifeboat disaster which shocked the country.

Elliot Galer

The *Elliot Galer* served as Seaham's lifeboat from 1911 until 1937. If the North Sea did not hold enough dangers for seafarers, the outbreak of war in 1914 brought new perils. Enemy warships and mines continually threatened local shipping.

On 21st August 1918 the steamer *The Stewarts Court* was torpedoed by the German submarine UB-112. At 2.45 in the afternoon the Lord Londonderry-owned *The Stewarts Court* was hit amidships. The explosion killed the Chief officer and broke the Master's leg. Within ten minutes the ship had gone down but not before the crew of 15 had taken to their lifeboat. The *Elliot Galer* picked the men up and landed them safely at Seaham Harbour.

Right and below: The *Elliot Galer* and crew.

The Lifeboat Disaster

A fishing trip from Seaham on Saturday 17th November 1962 ended in a tragedy that shook not only the town but the whole country.

The coble *Economy*, on a fishing trip with four men and a boy on board, began to take in water in rough seas. Seaham's lifeboat the *George Elmy* went to their aid. All were taken off and the lifeboat headed back to harbour. As it approached the piers the *George Elmy* was hit by two massive waves and overturned.

All five lifeboat crew: John Miller, Fred Gippert, James Farrington, Leonard Brown and Arthur Brown and four from the coble: Gordon Burrell, David Burrell, George Firth and Joseph Kennedy perished. The sole survivor was Donald Burrell who wrapped his arm around the propeller shaft to stay afloat. Tragically, his nine-year-old son David was one of those who died.

Above: The *George Elmy* returning to harbour a few years before the tragedy.

Right: The *George Elmy* washed ashore on Chemicals Beach the day after it was lost in going to the rescue of the coble *Economy*.

Seaham Harbour Lifeboat Disaster

Go to sleep little one
Though your daddy's far away
He lies asleep in a watery grave
In Seaham Harbour bay my son
In Seaham Harbour bay

In nineteen sixty-two
November gales did blow
And the rain battered down on the houses below
Yes down in this Earth below my son
Down on this Earth below

Then we heard the news
That out there on the sea
There are men and a boy in a little fishing coble
They call "Economy" my son
They call "Economy"

So with the lifeboat crew
Your daddy went to sea
'gainst storm and wind that sea to sail
In the bold "George Elmy" my son
In the bold "George Elmy"

And the sea it thundered and roared
But still your daddy sailed on
Sailed on 'till he reached those men and that boy
And got them safe on board my son
And got them safe on board

Then they turned about
And signalled to the land
"Our job is complete and we're coming home"
Safe from this salt sea foam my son
Safe from the salt sea foam.

But then that boat did lurch
Keeled over in the bay
Eight men and a boy in the cold cold sea
Were drowned that dreadful day my son
Were drowned that dreadful day

And one man lived to mourn
And one man lived to tell
Of the small boy who was drowned in the sea
Of the boy who was his son great God
The boy who was his son

Go to sleep little one
Though your daddy's far away
He lies asleep in a watery grave
In Seaham Harbour bay my son
In Seaham Harbour bay

A song written and performed by Ed Pickford

Ed Pickford on the cover of his album *The Song Writer* from which the *Seaham Harbour Lifeboat Disaster* is taken.

Ed also wrote the song *Oldest Swinger in Town* which Fred Wenlock had a Top Ten hit with in 1981.

Today Ed still performs his music in local folk clubs in his spare time.

Influenza

In the final months of the First World War a new menace struck which Seaham did not escape. An influenza epidemic claimed over twenty million lives around the world between April 1918 and May 1919. Most of the deaths were from pneumonia that followed the influenza attacks.

On the advice of the Medical Officer of Health, Seaham Urban District Council closed all elementary schools in the district to help stop the spread of the disease. In November 1918 one of Seaham's victims was William Davidson Dryden of Dene House Farm and Seaham Hall Farm. He died from pneumonia aged only 28, leaving a wife and four young children. He had taken over the farms only a few years before on the death of his father John.

In the winter of 1918 there were not enough men to dig the graves of influenza victims. Seaham UDC had to engage two men from the military as gravediggers during the epidemic.

The meeting of Seaham UDC of 4th April 1919 reported 33 deaths in the previous month and of these '12 of the deaths were due to influenza, and 5 from pulmonary diseases arising therefrom ... The influenza epidemic had now abated.'

Worldwide the influenza epidemic killed more people in one year than died in four years of fighting during the First World War.

TB & Diphtheria

When I was a child in the 1930s lots of people were dying of TB. There was also a diphtheria epidemic which claimed many of my friends. The little girl who sat next to me at school, Sylvia Flowerday, was one of its victims. How the rest of us escaped I don't know.

Joan Pace

Measles

Early this century, measles and whooping cough were still deadly diseases amongst Seaham children. In January 1907 a measles epidemic struck New Seaham then spread to Seaham Harbour. Many of the 400 cases were complicated by broncho-pneumonia. To try to stem the epidemic, the elementary schools were closed for six weeks and disinfectant supplied to the homes of infected houses. The measures helped bring the epidemic under control.

However, at a Council meeting it was reported there had been 13 deaths from measles in the district for the quarter ending 30th June 1907.

Help from the Neighbours

In the old days when men died in the pits the body used to be carried home on a door. It was laid out in the house of the mother or wife and a woman from the village would wash and prepare it. On the day of the funeral each of the neighbours brought something they had prepared. One would bake bread, another cakes, and another would prepare a tongue. This was because a family could not afford the funeral expenses as well as a wake.

Joan Pace

An advert from the *Seaham Observer* in 1858.

SECTION ELEVEN

THE WONDER OF WOOLWORTHS

Variety at Boggon's ... Cheap Potatoes ... Church Street ... Hutchinson's the Jewellers ... Woolies Comes to Town ... Forster's in Frances Street ... Saveloy Specials ... Wartime Coupons ... Broxholme's

Dicky Dido's in Church Street in 1998.

Boggon's

George Boggon's establishment in North Railway Street sold a wide variety of goods in the 1860s. The patent medicines include some that are still going strong after 130 years. Thomas Beecham had started making pills by hand in the 1840s and was later joined by his son Joseph. At the time of the advert (below) the pair were running the St Helens-based business with the help of only two boys. The firm grew into one of the largest drug companies in the country. Beecham's Powders are still a household name today.

BOOKBINDING in any style at
George Boggon's,
BOOKSELLER, PRINTER, AND STATIONER
27, NORTH RAILWAY STREET, SEAHAM
HARBOUR.

BIBLES, CHURCH SERVICES,
PRAYER BOOKS,
AND HYMN BOOKS,
CATHOLIC PRAYER BOOKS,
AT
Geo. Boggon's,
27, NORTH RAILWAY STREET,
SEAHAM HARBOUR.

PATENT MEDICINES

FRESH AND GENUINE
AT
GEORGE BOGGON'S
27, North Railway Street, Seaham Harbour.

HOLLOWAYS Pills,
Holloway's Ointment,
Beecham's Cough Pills,
Beecham's Patent Pills,
Cockle's Antibilious Pills,
Downie's Pills,
Parr's Life Pills,
Baxter's Tic. Pills,
Widow Welch's Pills,
Kay's Worsdell's Pills,
Page Woodcock's Wind Pills,
Locock's Pulmonic Wafers,
Powell's Balsam of Aniseed,
Mrs Winslow's Soothing Syrup,
Dalby's Carminative,
Abernethy's Gout Specific,
Baxter's Lung Preserver,
Turner's Tamarind Cough Emulsion,
Scott's Celebrated Oils,
Scott's Celebrated Drops,
Forster's Eureka Liniment,
Percy's Pectorial Balsam,
Blenkin's Pulmonic Elixir

CRICKET BATS, BALLS, STUMPS,
And every article connected with the game
can be had at
George Boggon's,
27, NORTH RAILWAY STREET,
SEAHAM HARBOUR.

An advert from the *Seaham Observer* in 1870

Adverts from the *Seaham Observer* in 1867.

Shopping Basket

In 1905 a 10 stone bag of potatoes could be had at J.G. Smith's shop at 8 Church Street for 3 shillings. A shilling bought you a dozen fresh farm eggs or a dozen duck eggs.

Church Street, Seaham Harbour. 5304

In 1923 *Ward's Directory* listed the shops in Church Street. These included: 7 grocers, 6 confectioners, 4 drapers, 3 boot dealers, 3 clothiers, 2 butchers, 2 fruiters, 2 milliners, 2 pharmacists, 2 pawnbrokers, 2 dairies, 2 tobacconists, a bank, tailor, picture framer, photographer, newsagent, saddler, pork butcher, fishmonger, painter, watch repairer, laundry, spirit merchant and undertaker. As well as these there were pubs, offices and a bazaar.

The pedestrianised Church Street of today does not quite have the quantity or variety of shops of the past.

E. & C. RYLES LTD

61 Princess Road
SEAHAM
County Durham

also at 46 Station Road
SEAHAM
County Durham

ICE CREAM of HIGHEST PURITY

Always at your Service   Our aim is to Serve you

**We cater for Dances,
Whist Drives and Celebrations**

HIGH CLASS CONFECTIONERS

Ryles' shop stood next to the Princess Theatre. Today it is private residence.

An advert from just after the last war. How many Seaham couples bought engagement and wedding rings at this Church Street jeweller?

Angus' butchers shop in Blandford Place. David Angus was co-author of the excellent *Seaham Harbour: The first 100 years 1828-1928* and *The Changing Face of Seaham 1928-1992.*

The Wonder of Woolworths

There used to be a Penny Bazaar in Church Street but it was very shabby. This was demolished and, wonder of wonders, Seaham had its own Woolworth's store. I distinctly remember going to Woolworth's with my sixpence for Christmas shopping. It was heaven.

Joan Pace

Seaham Harbour's very own Woolworth's store. 500 cubic feet of Crosland Hill Stone was used in its construction. This was supplied and erected in only five weeks by the Huddersfield firm of George Graham & Sons. The world famous department store built its reputation on nothing costing more than sixpence.

Church Street in an age when horse and cart was the main transport for delivery to and from shops.

Robert Forster's grocery and photographic shop in Frances Street in the 1920s. One of his specialities was coffee roasted daily.

Saveloy Specials

A treat on Saturday nights was going down the Harbour and being bought a penny saveloy or a two penny dip from one of the butchers shops in John Street. How things have changed when it comes to clothes and shoes. We had no say in the choice of what we would like to wear. The main criterion was that it should last a long time. All would be purchased at the Co-op. In those days we bought everything from the store. One of the reasons was the dividend which was given with each purchase. One of the first things us kids had to do was memorise the family's dividend number. I still remember our number after all these years – 1734.

George Forster

Below: Bill Brooks' fish shop in Church Street today.

Shops

Things like meat, milk and butter had to be bought almost daily because there were no storage facilities. We had a large stone slab in the pantry but this did not keep things fresh for long. Grocers seemed to flourish in Church Street – John George Smith was a high class grocer. There was a baker who sold Hovis bread made from Hovis flour. We thought that was something special. Broxholme's was a high class dress shop. When I think back the war ruined everything for some shops. When coupon rationing came in shops suffered.

Joan Pace

Right: An advert for Broxholme's store before the last war.

BROXHOLME'S

The Millinery Establishment,
Baby Linen Warehouse,
Ladies Underclothing Depot.
Corset Specialists.

Gloves.
    Ribbons.
        Flowers.
Furs.   Handkerchiefs.
   Scarfs.   Blouses.
   Art Needlework and Silks
      and Fancy Goods.

BROXHOLME'S

Fancy Drapers & Children's
Wear Specialists,

16 Church St. Seaham Harbour

While the birthrate might have fallen in Seaham in recent years, there is always a market for children's clothes shops like Andy Pandy's in Church Street.

CHURCH STREET, SEAHAM HARBOUR.

The People's History

To find out more about this unique series of local history books – and to receive a catalogue of the latest titles – send a large stamped addressed envelope to:

The People's History
Suite 1
Byron House
Seaham Grange Business Park
Seaham
County Durham
SR7 0PW